IS
SERIOUS
BUSINESS

A **Powerhouse Mindset**
FOR **SUCCESS**

CONNIE PODESTA

Happiness is Serious Business
A Powerhouse Mindset for Success
By Connie Podesta

Published by STANDOUT Press, Plano, Texas, USA

Printed in the United States of America.

Library of Congress Control Number: 2016917144

ISBN: 978-1-946225-00-9 (paperback)
       978-2-946225-01-6 (Kindle)
       978-1-946225-02-3 (ePub)

connie@conniepodesta.com
www.conniepodesta.com

DEDICATION

For my family and friends.
Happiness is having all of you in my life.

Connie

TABLE OF CONTENTS

SECTION THREE 98

The Tool to Dramatically Catapult Your Career

SECTION FOUR 150

The Prescription for Health and Well-Being

SECTION FIVE 180

The Secret to Personal Growth and Success

SECTION SIX 228

The Solution to Take Control of Your Life

@Connie_Podesta:

Behold the kick-butt power of Happiness. It can fuel your career and energize your life!

#ThePowerOfHappiness

It's Time to
TAKE
HAPPINESS
SERIOUSLY

Let me say it straight out. Happiness doesn't get the respect it deserves. Never has.

In some ways, I can understand why. It's rarely seen as a business power word. Ask people to describe the most in-demand traits of C-suite executives, high performers or strategic leaders, and you'll get responses like Success, Determination, Intelligence, Perseverance, Achievement, Integrity. Yes, all of those.

HAPPINESS doesn't even make the list.

1

What about job applicants? It's safe to say they aren't touting Happiness as one of their major strengths during interviews. Managers don't discuss Happiness during performance appraisals. And we certainly aren't seeing books on the business bestseller list titled *How to Create Happy Leaders* or *Making Happy Investments Work for You* or *Happy Sales Strategies for Success.*

Happiness just isn't viewed as the go-to feeling most people tap into in the midst of a storm, at work or at home. And yet, people tell me over and over again that, if they could have any one thing in life, it would be—you guessed it—more Happiness.

Happiness is the reason for everything, right? If we can't figure out how to be happy, then what's the point?

You've probably experienced Happiness many times in your life. But maybe you weren't always sure how to find it again. To keep it. To leverage it. Or how to tap into it when you need it the most.

Maybe it's time to just cut the crap and own up to the fact that HAPPINESS can be an undeniable power source that makes everything else we want possible. And it can be ours if we decide to change the way we look at it.

So here's the challenge.

Forget the idea that Happiness is a feeling that only emerges during the fun times. The nostalgic times. The times where we get what we want. And life goes as planned.

Happy moments?
Absolutely.

But I'm suggesting we adopt Happiness as a FULL-TIME, 24/7 STRATEGY. Pouring it into every crack and crevice between those major milestones. Even when life is messy, chaotic, or horribly painful. On weekdays and weekends. On good days and bad.

Does that sound crazy? Perhaps, but I'm going to change your mind.

Who am I, you ask, to tell you about Happiness? I've spent 30 years as a licensed professional counselor, therapist, international speaker, and executive coach. I've counseled, interviewed, coached, and spoken to more than 2 million people around the world. And worked with more than 1,000 organizations.

Believe me, I've heard all the stories. Witnessed every possible kind of relationship. Listened to all the excuses. Observed all the challenges. Watched all the sabotage. Celebrated hundreds of breakthroughs. And pushed, pulled, consoled, and cajoled people at every age and stage of life.

Don't worry. I've got your back. Nothing surprises me. Worries me. Or defeats me when it comes to helping YOU help yourself to be happier. Just keep reading. The chapters ahead will show you exactly why we all need to...

TAKE HAPPINESS MORE SERIOUSLY.

You'll quickly understand why the usual perceptions about Happiness are upside down and inside out. It's not an elusive, wimpy, weak emotion for people who aren't dedicated enough, independent enough, strong enough, or ambitious enough to man up and deal with life's challenges. Happiness isn't all cream puffs and "Kumbaya." Not by a long shot.

Nope. Happiness is tough as nails. Bullet-proof and unbeatable. A reality-based, in-your-face choice of emotion that can infiltrate adversity, reset trauma, and put a positive spin on setbacks with the force of a giant gladiator in your corner.

I realize that's a radically different way of thinking. But trust me, Happiness is a serious life strategy— with the potential to generate SERIOUS RESULTS for your career. Your life. Your health. Your relationships. And your future.

Are you ready to look at Happiness from a whole new angle?

Wait! Before you answer that, let's tackle the bigger question. How is your brain digesting the idea that

Happiness ranks up there with the likes of Power and Prosperity? Are you still reluctant to give Happiness a promotion and a corner office?

Here's the deal. If you have even the slightest bit of concern that a book on Happiness is venturing into the realm of motivational, rah-rah, personal-pompoms-in-the-air territory, think again.

I'm a research junkie. I'm all about the facts. And I'm still blown away by the fiercely compelling scientific data about...Happiness.

It's unexpected. But it's undeniable.

According to leading researchers at top institutions, a big dose of Happiness can help deliver enormous results:

- Live longer
- Make more money
- Strengthen the immune system
- Reduce stress
- Increase productivity
- Lose weight

- Sleep better
- Lower blood pressure
- Expand empathy
- Reduce the risk of disease
- Make more friends
- Decrease aches & pains
- Minimize anxiety
- Improve heart health
- Increase gratitude
- Achieve greater career success
- Build stronger relationships
- Recover faster from illness
- Become a better parent
- Change your life

Impressive list, right?

And they've got solid proof. I love that. Turns out, Happiness is a strikingly undervalued emotion with real, bottom-line impact and attention-grabbing ROI.

See what I mean? No room for doubt here.

HAPPINESS is the powerhouse mindset for SUCCESS.

This book will take you on an intriguing journey to explore the many facets and surprising angles of Happiness. Page by page, I'm going to convince you to take Happiness out of your "soft" list of nice things to have and move it to the top of your "how-to-get-the-life-and-success-you-deserve" list.

Are you ready?

You're about to see for yourself what Happiness can do for your career and your life. And why it's worth having. And fighting for.

Let's begin at the BEGINNING.

@Connie_Podesta:

Happiness is
serious business—
with big-time results.

#HappinessDeserves
Respect

HAPPINESS:
The **CATALYST** That Makes
SUCCESS POSSIBLE

Got your safety goggles? This section breaks down the key elements needed to activate your new perspective on Happiness. It's a critical shift in your viewpoint. One that will move your career forward while accelerating the pure joy in your life.

Oh, by the way...

You and Happiness? *Undeniable chemistry.*

Section 1

1

HAPPINESS
REDEFINED

One day it hit me. I finally figured out why everyone I counseled, coached, talked with, or interviewed desperately wanted to be happier. Across the board, Happiness was the ultimate (and seemingly unreachable) goal.

Sure, these people might have seen fleeting glimpses of Happiness at points in their lives, but then it was gone. They thought Happiness was sneaky. Tough to find. Even harder to grab and hold on to. For them, chasing Happiness was a full-time job with no paycheck.

I suddenly saw the problem: *their definition of Happiness was completely backwards.*

They believed Happiness was the aftereffect of accomplishments and accumulations.

Like most people, they had a mental list of all the stuff they needed, wanted, or expected to happen in their lives. Get the promotion. Afford the bigger house. Earn more money. Discover their soul mate. Purchase the latest iPhone. Lose weight. If they did those things, then they would be happy.

In the "if/then" equation of life, they saw Happiness as the consequence. No wonder Happiness is as elusive as a unicorn; it just doesn't work that way.

If this has been **your definition of Happiness,** it's time to flip it around.

OK, mind open. Heart ready. Brain engaged.

Here's the biggest secret you need to know:

HAPPINESS

is not the result of getting what you want; **it is the CATALYST that makes getting what you want possible.**

That's right, you heard me...

Happiness must come first!

Before we get what we want.

Radical concept, I know. Does that sound absurd? Counterintuitive to everything you've ever thought? Or heard? Or read? Or believed?

Maybe. But just think about this for a moment.

Section 1

We can't wait for Happiness to show up after all of our dreams come true. It's the dream maker. Happiness is what sets everything in motion. The beginning of the process. The strategic advantage. The secret sauce. The fuel that gets our success engines started.

Redefining Happiness in this way recognizes and validates the accountable part we each play in determining how happy we are. No waiting around for some special event or big milestone. Happiness is ready now; operators are standing by.

Still not convinced? Stay with me. I'm going to prove it—and give you plenty of reasons why changing the way you think about Happiness will change your life.

The following chapters are dedicated to expanding your new definition of Happiness. Giving it texture, context, and depth. The important background you need as you teach your mind to perceive Happiness differently. To adopt a new strategy. One that works for you, not against you.

Just wait.

You're going to LOVE the view of Happiness from this new angle.

@Connie_Podesta:

Redefine Happiness: it's the CATALYST that opens the door to endless possibilities!

#HappinessComesFirst

Section 1

2

HAPPINESS IS A POWERHOUSE MINDSET

As long as we think of Happiness as just an emotion or a feeling, we'll never uncover its true power. All we need to do is be willing and open to think about Happiness differently than we have before. From a totally unique perspective. Starting with mindsets and how they affect our lives.

So what is a mindset? And why is it so important?

A mindset is a group of assumptions, thoughts, beliefs, and attitudes that a person CHOOSES to adopt.

A mindset has the power to:
- **change behaviors,**
- **alter attitudes,**
- **affect moods,**
- and **impact actions...**

in either a positive or negative way. That's up to us.

Mindsets are potent. And they are rooted in CHOICE.

You might choose to adopt the mindset of a leader or entrepreneur. A community activist. An involved parent. Whatever it is, you get to pick.

No one was born with a mindset. We have to willingly invite it in. Welcome it. Nourish it. Support it. And allow it to determine the path we take. And the choices we make. In other words, our mindsets affect our future like nothing else can.

So, the most important question for you is: are you open to considering—*and perhaps adopting*—a new mindset when it comes to Happiness?

If so, your life is about to change forever.

@Connie_Podesta:

Happiness is a MINDSET that can change your life for the better.

#ThinkYourWayToHappy

Section 1

HAPPINESS
IS A **CHOICE**
FOR **SUCCESS**

With this new definition of Happiness, we have a CHOICE. And we never give up the power to control our own destinies.

Given any situation, we get to decide how to respond...

OPTION 1:
UNHAPPINESS

We can CHOOSE to believe we are POWERLESS and that life just happens to us. We can take the position that everything is out of our hands, and we don't have control over anything. We become the VICTIMS, simply REACTING with sadness, despair, hopelessness, and anger.

OPTION 2:
HAPPINESS

We can CHOOSE to believe we are POWERFUL and that our choices make a difference. We get to decide who we want in our lives, how we want to greet each day, and what our futures hold. We can choose not to let problems in the past (or naysayers in the present) rob us of our POTENTIAL. Our HOPE. Our HAPPINESS. We take the reins and go after what we want!

Just think how much more powerful, proactive, and purposeful we could be if we decided to view Happiness from this entirely new perspective—one that puts control back in our hands, even when facing tough challenges. Wouldn't that make life a bit easier?

Count me in for CHOICE and EMPOWERMENT, any day.

But often people say to me, "Connie, I didn't choose to get fired, to lose money on my investments, to get sick, or to have my spouse die or divorce me."

That's true.

Life throws us curveballs that were never in our plan for success.

I understand. Things happen that are so unfair we can hardly breathe. Sleep. Eat. Think. Move. I've been there. It sucks.

But then...it's up to us. The ball is in our court. We get to choose where it goes from there. We get to choose whether to ACT or REACT to the situation put before us.

If we decide to partner with Unhappiness, situations inevitably go from bad to worse. Unhappiness always chooses to ruin the relationship. Act out unkindly. Push loved ones away. Treat people badly. Make us feel like withdrawing and hiding.

On the other hand, HAPPINESS always chooses thoughtful, purposeful ACTION over angry, bitter, frustrated, irritated, and defeated REACTIONS. HAPPINESS is a powerful force to have on your side, no matter what the circumstances.

Why not make the power-packed choice to approach every situation from a foundation of Happiness?

It keeps YOU in control. And it's your best hope for building a better life and a stronger career.

@Connie_Podesta:

NEVER give up power to control your own destiny. Use Happiness to take the reins!

#HappinessIsAChoice

Section 1

HAPPINESS
Is Not An
INSURANCE POLICY

Choosing to adopt HAPPINESS as our go-to mindset is NOT a guarantee our lives will go smoothly or without incident, pain, loss, or disappointment. People get passed over for promotions. Kids get sick. Stock markets tumble. Computers crash. Unfortunately, those things are just part of life. No exemptions available.

Section 1

Hurt and sorrow make an unwelcome appearance in everyone's lives at some point. Even though HAPPINESS can't prevent the mishaps and disasters, it can be invaluable when painful emotions turn up on our doorsteps.

Yet, for many folks, when life does its thing and hands them a crisis, that's precisely when they give up on HAPPINESS. Push it away. Become afraid to experience it again. Let it be destroyed by uncertainty and difficulty. They stop fighting for Happiness. Instead, they begin to embrace UN-HAPPINESS, to accept it as their lot in life—and the choice changes everything from that moment on.

That's when UNHAPPINESS starts the cycle of creating and attracting even more of the things they did NOT want.

While HAPPINESS is NOT a guarantee that things won't go wrong, it is certainly the only mindset that has a shot at helping when life takes a turn for the worse. With a Happiness mindset, we'll be more prepared to handle the situation, resolve the problem, and cope with the collateral damage.

Honestly, HAPPINESS is like a life raft—it is there when we need it the most. It can't keep the storms away, but it can save us from drowning when we find ourselves in deep water.

IN CRISIS?

A Happiness mindset can help us see better, think more clearly, and find the best solution.

EXHAUSTED?

It gives us energy, pushes us to take care of ourselves, and turns fatigue into peace.

SCARED?

It brings us hope, challenges us to try new things, and gives us the courage to persevere.

SAD?

It lets us see things in perspective, creates an opportunity to think things through, and gives us a reason to work our way out of the sadness.

ANGRY?

It calms us down (if we'll let it), interjects some reason into our thoughts, and stops the blame game.

Section 1

HAPPINESS may not be an insurance policy against the many storms of life, but it can infuse a brilliant dose of sunshine to help you survive those dark days.

@Connie_Podesta:

Happiness is your life raft. It can't stop the storms, but it can save you from drowning.

#HappinessIsMyLifeRaft

5

HAPPINESS
IS A PRIVILEGE,
Not an Entitlement

HAPPINESS will never be a part of your life if YOU don't believe you DESERVE it.

Happiness is a courteous soul who waits patiently for a personal invitation from YOU and won't ever crash your party. This is YOUR life, YOUR choice. Consequently, YOU must first believe with every fiber of your being that YOU—yes, YOU—are a worthwhile individual who DESERVES to have HAPPINESS as a foundation for success in your life and your career.

And why stop there? Let's throw this in while we're at it:

You also **deserve to be** LOVED. RESPECTED. APPRECIATED. RECOGNIZED. And **TREATED FAIRLY.**

But here's the fine print: "deserve" does NOT mean "entitled to."

We are absolutely not *entitled* to Happiness, respect, and the rest of the gang.

Entitlement means believing we are owed Happiness and love and respect and recognition without doing the work it takes to earn them. No way! Not going to happen. Just saying.

Happiness and its elite friends are privileges. And privileges must be earned.

They are available to us if we want them badly enough. And if we are willing to go after them. Do the work. And fight every step of the way. Otherwise, we won't have them in our lives. Simple as that.

Happiness, respect, and appreciation are hard enough to get even when we are doing everything in our power to make them happen. They aren't automatic. Why? Because no one owes us anything.

If we want good things, we have to go fight for them. Work for them. Earn them. Put in the overtime.

Unfortunately, that's a problem for many folks. We are living in quite the entitled nation right now. People want the results without the work. They gripe about being unhappy, but they do nothing to change the course of their lives, their plans, or their mindsets.

They complain about others being lucky, without looking inward to see how they might be sabotaging their own success. Like the guy who complains that he has never won the lottery, only to be reminded that he never buys a ticket.

You must be willing to buy the ticket to your own success.

Are you fighting to be HAPPY or UNHAPPY? Are you your best friend or your worst enemy? Do you help yourself or sabotage yourself?

I promise you that GREAT things are out there, but you have to SHOUT OUT that you are ready, willing, and able to do what it takes. Don't give up. Make it a PRIORITY.

Forget entitlement. Start earning the privilege of Happiness.

READY?

@Connie_Podesta:

You absolutely DESERVE Happiness. When you choose it. And work for it.

#ThePrivilegeOf Happiness

6

HAPPINESS
Knows How and When
TO QUIT

HAPPINESS is all about quitting.

Wait, what?!?

You heard me. That sounds counterintuitive in a world where the common mantras are:

> *"Hang in there."*
> *"Never give up."*
> *"Stick with it."*

HAPPINESS never asks you to quit just because life isn't fair. Or work gets a bit stressful. Or a relationship is going through the usual tough times.

It won't ask you to quit because you want to avoid hard truths. Or have to make tough decisions. And it will definitely not ask you to quit just so you can take the easy way out.

HAPPINESS pushes you to quit the...
- **mindsets,**
- **attitudes,**
- **behaviors,**
- **and actions...**

that are getting in the way of creating the best possible life for you and those you care about.

So many times, we desperately try to hold on to things that are NOT at all happy, healthy, or in our best interests. Bad jobs. Toxic relationships. Old habits. Sad memories. Hurtful experiences. Jealousy. Worry. Grief. Loving someone who doesn't love us back. Futile attempts to change other people.

The would-haves, should-haves, could-haves. Opportunities we wished we had taken. Things we should have done differently. Children we should have spent more time with. Words we wish we hadn't said. The "good old days" or the way it "used to be."

So what's that all about? In psychology, we refer to it as…

"FIGHTING FOR OUR LIMITATIONS."

That means fighting to hang on to what is keeping us down, tearing us apart, distracting us from reality, and pulling us away from what we need to succeed—namely, HAPPINESS. Why would anyone do that?

Because letting go can be scary. But I promise you this: holding on is sucking the creative, positive, productive energy right out of your body and soul. Letting go is about HOPE, FORGIVENESS, and the refusal to be weighed down by worry, guilt, and second-guessing.

Letting go is wildly liberating.

Tell yourself: it is what it is...at this moment. The past is gone, and the future is still YOURS. When you decide to let go of everything that is keeping you from moving ahead, you can be focused and determined to SUCCEED. You will find the new job, a better business opportunity, or more compatible "significant other."

So figure out what is holding you back. What thoughts keep going through your mind that you need to shake? What people cause you sadness and stress? What negative self-talk sabotages you from the inside out?

Keep telling yourself that Unhappiness holds on to everything so tight that, over time, it will crush your brain, weaken your soul, stamp out your ambition, and destroy your heart. LET GO of the things and people that make you unhappy.

And by the way, it's critical to let go of Unhappiness in real life—and on social media. You can't really let go when you are still following Unhappiness on

Twitter and Instagram. If you want to fully block out the negativity, seal up all of the cracks so it can't sneak back in.

Now. Take a deep breath.

HAPPINESS will take over and propel you ahead—just give it a chance. Trust me. When you do, your mind will SOAR!

@Connie_Podesta:

Happiness lets GO of old hurt, old haunts, old habits.

#LetGoChoose Happiness

Section 1

7

HAPPINESS
IS WORTH
THE FIGHT

Happiness definitely isn't for wimps. Or the faint of heart. It takes courage and determination to choose Happiness as our teammate. Advisor. Partner. Companion. Mentor. Friend.

Why? Because it's the tougher battle. It's a fight. Not a bold disagreement, but a prime-time showdown where we'd better put on our boxing gloves and step into the ring.

That's why many people have decided it is easier, much easier, to just let Unhappiness rule the day than to do what it takes to keep Happiness alive and well.

Sooner or later, life is going to knock all of us down with tough circumstances. It's hard to have a cheery disposition when the news is filled with stories about crime and violence and tragedy. Or when our product strategy fails, our market share tanks, and our budgets are slashed. Ready to fight back? Oh no, the path of least resistance is curling up in the corner with Unhappiness as our big, heavy, miserable blanket.

Trust me. I have first-hand experience with the fight-for-Happiness struggle, most recently when I had a serious house fire. I found myself once again standing at the crossroads of Happiness and Unhappiness. As I watched the firefighters—knowing there was nothing I could do and no way to recover all of the things I loved—Unhappiness was beckoning me to give up and give in.

My emotions were all over the place. It was heartbreaking to realize that our home was essentially gone, along with everything inside. I was angry thinking about the faulty electrical wiring and what should have been done to prevent the fire. Top that off with overwhelming dread about what was ahead for us—a year of rebuilding and putting our lives back together.

In the midst of all that Unhappiness, I knew that I needed to take my own advice. I could not let sadness and anger rule the day. If I was going to get through this, I needed to grab onto some Happiness.

Really?
HAPPINESS?

A dumpster sat in my driveway. Men were hauling away my possessions, now unrecognizable. My computer and all my records had been destroyed, but I had to keep my business going. Sure, I'll focus on Happiness...

Whew. Not an easy task.

But as I thought more about the situation, I did detect some gratitude. We all made it out of the burning house alive and safe, even the pets. The firefighters worked hard to help us save whatever they could. Our neighbors' homes were not affected. And we had only lost material things— almost all of them replaceable. Yes, these were definitely things to be happy about.

Happiness was actually right there in the smoldering rubble.

So I fought. Every day. To find a tiny sliver of resilience. To regain a sense of balance. To discover some rays of hope. To not lose touch with who I was. And to begin the process of recovering.

In the months ahead, I fought for Happiness to carry me through. I smiled (not so easy at first). I worked closely with the people rebuilding. Thanked them endlessly. Brought them sandwiches at lunch. Gave them hugs as they completed each step. Had a great relationship with my insurance agent, as well as my general contractor.

And guess what? Everyone worked extremely hard and stayed extra-long hours. The house was rebuilt in record time. In fact, my general contractor said, "I have never seen my guys enjoy working on a job so much. Or a rebuild go so smoothly."

That's the power of Happiness. Toss in a healthy dose of gratitude, and it's an unstoppable combination. By fighting to keep Happiness in our corner after the fire, we attracted a great team, willing and able to help us every step of the way.

This is just one example of how Happiness can give you a giant head start on recovery, even in the very worst of times. It gives us the strength to get through them. To find meaning and purpose again.

Happiness is the amazing medicine that makes it possible. The sought-after antidote. The eons-old remedy for what ails us. Hurts us. Takes us down. And derails us.

But we have to make room for it. And want it. And believe we deserve it.

It's always worth the fight.

@Connie_Podesta:

Happiness isn't easy.
But it's worth fighting for!

#FightForHappiness

HAPPINESS:
The **Mindset** That
CHANGES
EVERYTHING

Choosing Happiness is like watching a movie in IMAX 3D after you've been struggling to see it on your iPhone screen. With bad Wi-Fi. Vastly different experience.

This section premieres the blockbuster impact of Happiness. How it works. How it affects your professional trajectory. What it means for everyday living. And why you'll definitely give it two thumbs up.

It's going to be epic. Now pass the popcorn.

Section 2

1

HAPPINESS
ATTRACTS
GOOD THINGS

Happiness is like a gigantic MAGNET that reaches out and attracts all sorts of great things. People. Jobs. Success. Friends. Partners. Opportunities.

So how does that work exactly?

We already know that Happiness is a CHOICE. And choosing which thoughts, attitudes, and beliefs we allow into our lives plays a HUGE role in whether or not we get what we want and reach our goals.

That's because...

Our thoughts and beliefs turn into ACTIONS and BEHAVIORS.

And those behaviors (verbal and nonverbal) are visible for the world to see. Feel. React to. Pick up on. Accept. Pull away from. Agree with.

Our actions and behaviors also determine how people treat us. Whether people trust us. Want to be with us. Hire us. Work for us. Live with us. Buy from us. Believe in us. Help us. Partner with us.

No genius at work here. It's just the way it is. When our attitude of Happiness translates into our behaviors, we are helping to shape a positive outcome.

The problem is, Unhappiness is a magnet as well. It scoops up and attracts bad stuff—and usually at the very moment we need a break from adversity.

For example, when we are angry, we tend to attract other angry people. When we don't do the work, we lose the job. When we make bad decisions that are not in our own best interests, we end up paying the price. And yada yada yada.

Sure, we're still shaping our own outcomes, but they arrive in the form of negative consequences.

When Unhappiness triggers a downward spiral and things go astray, we are left with no effective coping skills to solve the problem. No positive spirit to help us through. No creative ideas to get us going. No support system to push us forward. No confidence that we can do what it takes. And no hope that things will get better. Unhappiness only sees what cannot be done.

Well, that paints a bleak picture, huh?

Don't panic yet: **there is good news.**

We get to DECIDE which magnet to turn on. What we want to ATTRACT into our lives. Who we want to associate with. How we want to spend our time.

Notice the parallel there? Happiness is all about choice. Don't you love that?

Bottom line:

People like to **be around** HAPPY PEOPLE.

They also like to:
- Hire them.
- Work with them.
- Promote them.
- Marry them.
- Partner with them.
- Live with them.
- Buy from them.
- Learn from them.
- Support them.
- And do good things for them.

It's just common sense. And it also explains why we can't wait to be happy until AFTER we get what we want. If we're unhappy while we are trying to reach all of our goals, what are the odds that we'll be successful?

The truth is, unhappy people don't usually get hired for great jobs. Or attract their perfect soul mates. Or make lots of new friends. Unhappiness pushes away everything good in their lives. And puts them even further away from the things they want.

One of my clients discovered this concept the hard way. Meagan *(not her real name)* lost her job due to cutbacks. These things happen; we've all been there.

But Unhappiness invaded.

It permeated every part of her life. Her mood. Her spirit. Her relationships. Her health. By the time she came to me for coaching, her life was worse than ever. I noticed it the minute she walked in. Shoulders drooped. No spark in her eyes. No excitement radiating from her.

Her first comment confirmed my observations.

> *"I can't believe it. After all I've been through, my life just continues to get worse day by day. How much longer is my bad luck going to continue?"*

My answer was direct:

> *"I can tell you exactly! It's going to last until you find a way to bring some Happiness into your life."*

She looked at me as though I were crazy.

As we started to unpack her troubles, we quickly discovered a common culprit behind all of them.

Meagan had experienced a legitimate setback with the job layoff. Not her fault. Not her choice. But that's when Unhappiness saw its chance. To move in, get settled, and attract even more Unhappiness into her life.

How did that go over at her job interviews? Not a great impression. Yes, she answered their questions. But she didn't come up with any compelling ideas. She wasn't proactive about sharing what she could bring to the table. No connections with the people interviewing her, and no job offers.

What about her health? Well, Unhappiness loves to eat junk food. Meagan had unknowingly sabotaged all of her efforts to stay trim. She justified eating those calorie-laden comfort foods because she was so unhappy. Her weight went up, her energy level plummeted, and the nagging fatigue overwhelmed her.

How about her boyfriend? Confused and frustrated. Meagan had been distant and downright prickly in the past few months. Hard to reach. Difficult to talk to. And seldom affectionate. Which explains why he started to seem withdrawn and uninterested.

As Meagan and I worked together, she began to recognize the thread of Unhappiness weaving throughout the fabric of her life. She was ready for change, even if it looked like an uphill battle.

"Search for Happiness," I told her. "Go get it, and don't give up. It's out there. You just haven't been fighting to bring it back into your life. Be excited you have an interview. Be grateful you have someone you love and who loves you. Be thankful you have the know-how to make smart food choices.

You might have to 'act' happy at first. But do it, and watch what happens almost immediately."

Sure enough, after three more interviews, Meagan landed a great job. Without effort, she stopped eating to make up for her disappointments. Her enthusiasm for life returned. Her boyfriend was thrilled that the warm, lovable Meagan was back. He even celebrated by surprising her with a long, romantic weekend out of town.

Meagan's Happiness attracted more Happiness. And Unhappiness got an eviction notice.

That's it.

That's the **magical, super-cool part** of **HAPPINESS.**

When we make the choice to purposefully embrace Happiness as our go-to mindset, we begin to attract the things we want. Need. And deserve.

Even when life throws us for a loop, Happiness will steer us to ACT with confidence, not REACT as victims. There's almost nothing we can't do, change, resolve, cope with, handle, understand, forgive, or embrace when we come from a place of Happiness.

Now, isn't that attractive?!

@Connie_Podesta:

Happiness positions you to attract great things into your life, shaping your future in amazing ways!

#TheHappinessMagnet

Section 2

2

HAPPINESS
BALANCES OUT
EVERYTHING

Balance is a tough concept in today's chaotic world.

Research says 80% of people are never more than five feet away from their cell phones. I'm guessing the other 20% are glued to their laptops or tablet computers. The technology addiction is real, and moderation isn't the norm.

We all face constant change. Longer work hours, less sleep, and fewer vacation days.

We're distracted by our personal lives while we're at the office. And we're distracted by our business deadlines when we're at home. If only we had better time management skills...

Nope. Sound the annoying buzzer. That's not the solution at all.

Bottom line:
We CANNOT manage time.

We can only manage how we CHOOSE to use the time we have.

Begin by
REDEFINING
BALANCE.

Here's the reality:

You don't have a professional life and a personal life—you have a LIFE!

Achieving balance isn't about allotting equal time to the standard sections of our days. 8 hours in the office. 8 hours with the family. 8 hours sleeping (minus whatever we lose in that daily battle with the snooze button…).

Balance is about having a sense of well-being, fulfillment, respect and, of course, HAPPINESS in our lives at all levels. At all times. At work and at home. When we're in line at the grocery store. Making the big presentation. Getting our teeth cleaned.

Yep, Happiness is a 24/7, EQUAL OPPORTUNITY EMOTION.

If we choose Happiness, it will go with us everywhere. A nice sidekick, don't you agree?

HAPPINESS also puts balance into a recognizable perspective and offers us the reward of freedom. Freedom from trying to "have it all."

Freedom of knowing when "enough is enough." Freedom to keep moving forward in our lives at the pace we set, no matter what. Now that's true freedom.

And what about the villain who wants to destroy our balance? UNHAPPINESS plants the seeds deep inside our brains and hearts that we can and must DO IT ALL. And more. It allows guilt to fester if we can't handle everything. In fact, Unhappiness is at the root of the myth that multi-tasking is a good trait. It is not!

My research shows that multi-tasking doesn't make us more efficient. It simply takes us off task and creates a craziness around us that's hard to overcome. Do you feel your heart racing? Your temper rising? Your irritability showing? Your confidence plummeting because there's still more to do? Do you feel as if you are running a race that you can never finish?

Wait a second...that's UNHAPPINESS having its way with you. Don't believe the myth; multi-tasking can have serious, negative side effects.

Take a breath.
Seriously, take a breath. Now another.

Think about what you're doing. The purpose behind your task. What is this all about? Who is all of this for? Why do you define your life by how fast you work? Why is your worth measured by how little time you have left for yourself?

I hear people bragging all the time about how little they sleep. How long it's been since they took a vacation. Or how late they stayed up. As if these were positive traits. Really?

Scratch that. These are negative, get-sick-soon, miss-out-on-the-beauty-of-life traits. Being able to say "I DID THE MOST" is not a great competition to win. Could people actually want that to be their legacy?

HAPPINESS knows that sometimes the best thing we can do for ourselves and the people in our lives is to just STOP. Give ourselves a break. Nurture our own spirits. Take care of our own hearts. There are times we get so caught up in taking care of the world that we forget to take care of ourselves.

67

"Oh," you say, "I'm just too busy. No time today."

I don't buy it! Every day has a few wasted moments doing silly, totally unnecessary stuff, right? Start today to make those minutes count—for YOU, your family, your health, your career, and your future.

People often ask how they can achieve more balance in their lives. Start here.

Just for TODAY, let HAPPINESS take care of you— even if it's only for a few minutes. (The world will be OK for a little while...no worries!)

Let it go.

@Connie_Podesta:

Embrace the balance: you don't have a professional life and a personal life— you have a LIFE!

#HappinessIsBalanced

3

HAPPINESS
IS FEARLESS

FEARLESSNESS!

What a fabulous concept.

But it may be different than you think. Being FEARLESS doesn't mean you aren't afraid. Worried. Intimidated. Reluctant. Cautious. Or sometimes, even downright scared to death.

Let's face it.

Life can be scary no matter how confident and tough we are.

It's normal to get that pit in our stomachs when we hear about the reorganization rumors, the high failure rate on the certification test, or the dreaded results of a medical exam. That's just part of the journey.

So what is the difference between being FEARFUL and FEARLESS, really?

FEARFUL people
are afraid and then...choose to do NOTHING.

They use fear as an excuse to avoid action.

FEARLESS people
are afraid and then...take ACTION.

They fight the fear so they can move beyond it. Understand it. Deal with it. Learn from it. Leverage it. OVERCOME IT.

FEARFUL PEOPLE use their fears as excuses to stay paralyzed in a state of inactivity. They use their fears as reasons to become territorial, resist change, avoid crucial conversations, display negative attitudes, blame others or the economy or anything they can think of for their misfortune, to deny accountability, become complacent, and fight to keep the status quo. They use their fears as justification for not standing up and taking action.

Fearful people invite Unhappiness right smack inside the front door. Unhappiness provides the shelter and nourishment that fear needs. And then Unhappiness becomes fear's constant companion.

Unhappiness breeds fear. And vice versa. Unhappy people are afraid to let go. Change patterns. Try a different approach. All of which creates even more distress. And even more fear. Ugh!

FEARLESS PEOPLE are afraid at times, too. It can definitely be a frightening world. For all of us. But here's the difference. Fearless people are afraid and then...they move forward anyway. They CHOOSE to use their fears as a catalyst to become stronger, fight harder to understand, initiate fresh ideas, invent new solutions, deal with change quickly and effectively, and forge ahead into unknown territory.

So which path do you want to take? What kind of person do you want to be?

Remember, fears are...

Exacerbated by inaction.
Propelled by insecurity.
Driven by indecisiveness.
Fueled by worry.

Fears exist in all of us. It's HOW we react to those fears that determines the direction our lives take. We can hide behind them. Or move out in front of them. We can give them power. Or take power over them. We can use them as an excuse. Or use them as a kick in the butt.

Again, it is OUR choice. But I can promise you one thing: choosing a mindset of HAPPINESS definitely helps create a stronger sense of FEARLESSNESS because of its very nature.

HAPPINESS empowers us to be more decisive, creative, loving, productive, innovative, and optimistic. It ATTRACTS the kinds of people into our lives who can help us overcome fears when they present themselves. People who have known fear and conquered it.

Happiness arms us with the courage we need to overcome setbacks. And to get beyond our hesitation and into take-charge action. HAPPINESS helps us leverage every asset we have to face whatever comes our way!

Are you ready to stop being pushed and pulled by fear, and to start making decisions from a place of confidence and success? Then let HAPPINESS show you the way.

@Connie_Podesta:

Fearful? Make HAPPINESS your suit of armor. You'll feel braver and calmer with it on.

#FearlesslyHappy

Section 2

4

HAPPINESS
Keeps You **Living**
IN THE PRESENT

UNHAPPINESS would love for us to mentally exist in the past. But take note: our past is NOT who we ARE. Our past in no way defines us as people at this moment or our potential for success in the future.

The past is just a compilation of the experiences we have had—some good, some not-so-good.

But we are so much more. More than any set of circumstances.

Most people have experienced things in life that weren't fair. Things that were said and done that are hard to forgive or forget. I know. I've been there. And so have my friends.

One of my clients named Kevin *(not his real name)* was sharp, talented, and hard working. Great qualities that still didn't save him from Unhappiness. He seemed endlessly stuck in the quicksand of the past with no apparent hope of breaking free.

Instead of using his diverse skills to create a successful future, he spent all of his time rehashing lost opportunities. Failed relationships. Stupid decisions. Bad situations he couldn't change. Things that happened on a calendar page long since turned. Old news.

But Kevin couldn't let them go. And his enormous potential was trapped right there with him.

The same tragic thing can happen to us. If we let past experiences define us, we're focused on who we WERE. Not who we ARE now. Much less, who we WANT TO BE.

What's the answer? To let those people, circumstances, history, or habits have ALL the power? Are we going to let what happened in the past rob us of what could be or should be in our future?

Fortunately, Kevin was ready to move forward. He decided to step up, live in the present, and choose HAPPINESS!

Like Kevin, you might not be able to control the past. But the good news is, the future is right there in your own sweet little hands.

You are IN CHARGE of NOW.

Know this:

No one is responsible for the rest of your life but YOU.

You make the CHOICES. YOU have the POWER and the POTENTIAL for ANYTHING.

Let the past be a source of lessons, and then let it GO! Focus on the PRESENT! And fight for your right to be happy now—and in the future.

@Connie_Podesta:

Your past? NOT who you are now. Learn from the lessons, and move on with Happiness.

#HappyFromHereOnOut

5

HAPPINESS
IS HOPE

Unhappiness would love to steal our hope right out from underneath us. And lock it away, losing the key. Why? Because hope is the reason we can keep going, living, learning, growing, leading, creating, and existing when times are difficult and life isn't fair.

UNHAPPINESS's best friend—despair—never attracts good things into our lives. Which makes it the polar opposite of hope.

Hope is believing in the midst of fear that we can forge ahead and find our way.

In times of sorrow or sadness that we can still be open to new relationships, anticipate a better ending, expect things to change for the better, or believe what is wanted or needed can be obtained.

In the midst of **DESPERATION,** HAPPINESS fills us with a sense of hope.

A feeling that helps us embrace the strong possibility that we will find solutions that could lead us out of despair and hopelessness. Perhaps even into new, exciting, and different directions.

Hope means that, for each and every problem, there is another way, another answer, another job, another person to love, another idea, another place, another path—another opportunity to help us move on.

Hope is about believing we are designed to hit roadblocks, but knowing we have the capacity to find detours and continue moving toward our goals.

Hope is trusting there is a way—some way—out of this. Hope means NOT giving up on ourselves.

And the truth is...

Hope and HAPPINESS walk hand in hand, especially in tough times. That's when a mindset of HAPPINESS begins to really do its job and kick in. It's what tells HOPE to fill our minds and hearts with all of the possibilities that can turn bad times into good.

I love that. Don't you?

@Connie_Podesta:

Happiness walks hand in hand with HOPE. To find SOLUTIONS. Create ENERGY. Get us to the other side.

#TheHappySideOfHope

Section 2

6

HAPPINESS DOESN'T PROCRASTINATE

"Nooooo! Not today. Can't I just think about that tomorrow?"

Sound familiar?

UNHAPPINESS loves it when we delay tough projects and decisions. Put things off. And avoid what we don't like to do. Why?

Because delaying things makes us feel bad about ourselves. And it causes stress. And worry. And anxiety. And let me assure you, UNHAPPINESS loves it when we are super stressed and loaded with anxiety.

Want to give Unhappiness a real thrill?

Wait to start your taxes until April 14th. Avoid backing up your computer for six months. Postpone updating your passport until 48 hours before your international flight.

Let there be no doubt, procrastination is the silent killer of ambition, productivity, achievement, even peace and balance. And most importantly, it undermines our own HAPPINESS. Putting things off causes more stress, worry, and insecurity about the future than just taking a deep breath and completing the first step.

There are many ways to procrastinate. Some people simply choose to do NOTHING—except maybe fret, worry, feel guilty, and stress out. Doing absolutely NOTHING instead of CHOOSING to make the first move definitely comes from a place of UNHAPPINESS.

Another way people procrastinate is by doing other things that are totally unimportant—things that are useless, silly, low priority, meaningless—in an attempt to convince themselves they are indeed BUSY. Busy doing what, really? Busy stressing and being unhappy? For sure!

Procrastination in any form is deadly when we are actually seeking progress, learning, development, creativity, and problem solving. At work, at home, wherever we go.

So if this concept resonates with you, I'll take a wild guess at your next thought.

> *"I know I procrastinate, and I really need to do something about that. Next week."*

I challenge you to fight that naturally ingrained delay tactic. Just dive in, and try to gain some momentum. Getting started is the hardest part, but it's all downhill from there.

Where to begin?
ANYWHERE.

Honestly, just start anywhere. When I find myself trying to avoid something, I look for the easiest place to start. The cheapest. The least frightening. The most accessible. The least painful. The most comfortable. And then I begin to work my way forward. Inch by inch.

If you're putting all of the big stuff OFF day after day, I am here to tell you that you are seriously causing yourself more anxiety and slowly eroding your self-esteem and feelings of self-worth and fulfillment.

Don't wait for tomorrow, next year, the new job to start, the kids to be grown, the economy to change, or your ship to come in. Make today the day YOU GET STARTED—one step at a time. Happiness will keep pushing you forward.

You can do it. I promise.

And it will feel incredible!

@Connie_Podesta:

Procrastination is the silent killer of ambition, productivity, peace, and balance.

#HappinessDivesIn

Section 2

7

HAPPINESS, THY NAME IS COURAGE

HAPPINESS knows it takes COURAGE to really go after what we want, stepping off that ledge into the uncertain, unpredictable, and unknown. Applying for the dream job. Approaching an industry icon to be a mentor. Running for a political office. Agreeing to the blind date. Deciding to move to another country.

Frightening? Oh yeah!

Worth it?

ABSOLUTELY.

People ask if I am nervous before I walk on stage to speak. You bet! Every single time.

Then they ask why I keep doing it. And I tell them it's because the results are so worth the butterflies. The point is, nothing amazing is ever done without nerves, a little fear here and there, and a knot in the stomach that says...

"Seriously? Are you really going to do this?"

And the **answer is...**

"You bet I am."

I appreciate the butterflies. They make me realize I am not taking life for granted one little bit. That each client is important. That each person I meet is important. That every decision I make is important. That I am important. Important enough to want to make sure I get it right. Do the right thing. Be the best I can be.

The opposite of this jangle of excited nerves is complacency. And that is a dull, uninspired, and even dangerous place to be.

Complacency can take away a job. Kill a marriage. Zap your energy and creativity. Allow you to be satisfied with the status quo. Cause you to give up fighting to be everything your incredible self can be.

The jitters are just the price we pay to appreciate the things we love, be with the people we love, have the job we love. No one said it would be easy. But the results?

Pretty darn AMAZING!

@Connie_Podesta:

Chasing your dreams? Happiness gives you the courage to go for it!

#HappinessIsCourage

Section 2

8

HAPPINESS
IS HAPPILY
FLAWED

Perfection?

Overrated. Unreachable. Exhausting. Impossible. Obsessive. Look, I'm not saying we should stop reaching for more. Striving for excellence. Far from it. But no one—NO ONE—is perfect.

Happiness is getting to that point in your life where you can say...

"I don't have to have it all, do it all, be the best."

And genuinely being OK with that.

There's a very real difference between "getting it perfect" and "giving it all you have." Happiness is about realizing mistakes are part of life's crazy plan so we can learn how to do better next time.

Unhappiness is about never being satisfied, a constant need for overachieving, and setting goals so high we can never win. That's a big plate of frustration with a side of disappointment.

HAPPINESS knows that LIFE IS A JOURNEY with ups and downs

—and that's just fine! We can handle it and figure it out as we go along.

HAPPINESS is never self-critical.

It does, however, have expectations about our performance.

It won't let us get away with doing sloppy work. Or not giving it our all. Or giving up without trying. It will call us out on those things. For sure.

But HAPPINESS doesn't keep up a conversation inside our heads all day long about what an idiot we were in the meeting. Or keep replaying over and over the stupid things we did. Or said. Or sent in a rash text message. It doesn't make us feel ashamed. Or worthless. Or stupid.

Oh no, that's UNHAPPPINESS sticking its nose in where it doesn't belong.

HAPPINESS cares more about what we think about ourselves than what others think of us. It doesn't NEED others to approve of us. Love us. Want us. Need us. Because HAPPINESS is comfortable within itself. As long as we choose HAPPINESS, we have a friend.

So what's the big take-away for you?

HAPPINESS accepts your imperfections. And uses them to make you more real. More accessible. Less judgmental. Remember, attraction starts with YOU.

You must love yourself and be loving to attract love. Respect yourself before you attract respect. Accept yourself for who you are—including your flaws—before others can embrace you. Believe in you. And trust you.

You can't and won't always be everything to everyone. UNHAPPINESS will have you constantly searching for perfection—which can become very addictive. Very annoying. And very unproductive.

Give yourself a break. You'll be glad you did. Let HAPPINESS in and find out how wonderful self-acceptance can be.

@Connie_Podesta:

Celebrate your flaws, imperfections, and differences! They make up the special person that is YOU!

#HappinessIsntPerfect

HAPPINESS:
The Tool to
DRAMATICALLY
CATAPULT
YOUR
CAREER

Want to measurably build up your professional success? Or maybe repair some damage? Happiness is the serious power tool you need. This section drills down to show how Happiness can help you renovate your career and rewire your performance, all with stunning results.

No duct tape required.

Section 3

1

HAPPINESS
IS JOB
SECURITY

Let's talk about work for a minute. Most people don't rank HAPPINESS as a major component of success in the workplace. How many times do people list "I'm so happy" as a skill on their résumés? I've never seen it. Not even once.

Is your "Happiness level" ranked on the evaluation sheet that determines your annual raise or promotion? Are you attending training workshops on "Raising the Bar for Happiness" or "Exceeding

Happiness Expectations"? Does your company have a five-year strategic plan for increasing Happiness ratios? Probably not.

But let me tell you this:

HAPPINESS literally ROCKS the workplace...

...in terms of making money, boosting success, increasing customer base, closing more deals, and expanding market share. And talk about ROI!

Happiness is like the investment that never goes down in value. Believe me, in a world where competition is tough, products look alike, prices are similar, and change happens at the click of a mouse, our best shot at success is to differentiate ourselves and literally...

STAND OUT FROM THE CROWD
in a positive way—by being happy.

After interviewing thousands of CEOs, HR directors, and business owners, I found a common denominator in all of their responses:

"We can teach skills, but we don't have the time or energy to turn a negative, unhappy person with a bad attitude into a happy, willing, creative, and productive worker."

In other words...

the UNHAPPY PEOPLE have to go.

So the leaders start to plot and plan how to get rid of unhappy people (or move them to a competitor) as soon as possible. The exit interview might include a range of feedback, but likely not the truth:

"You were simply too unhappy to be around."

The bottom line...

Life is too hard and too busy for people to have to work for or beside anyone who radiates doom and gloom.

Just saying.

Often people tell me...

> *"Connie, no one has a right to tell me that I have to be happy at work."*

No, but they certainly have a right to expect you to act happy while on paid work time.

Why? For very good reasons. An unhappy mindset decreases your productivity. Negatively impacts your ability to share, collaborate, and work well as a team. It reduces your creativity. Lowers your resilience. It sucks the energy right out of your body. And it quickly spreads.

Everyone around an unhappy person loses energy. How many employers want a negative attitude hanging around their offices? Or their customers?

No calculator needed here. The answer is none of them. Ever. Not one.

There's another objection that frequently comes up.

"Connie, if I acted happy, that would be phony."

No, it would not be. Acting happy is acting professional. You are at work to support your team, help your customers, find solutions, make profits—not to bring people into your personal drama. Save that for your best friend or your therapist.

Hands down, I'd go for the Happiness "act" without hesitation. And guess what? My thirty years of experience have shown that people who "act" happy end up truly feeling happier. What a deal!

If you want to attract the best customers, the leading companies, the smartest deals, the most sought-after jobs, and the most amazing opportunities, Happiness is the key. Your personality has to reflect a positive spirit.

HAPPINESS is your best chance for job security—

because it's bigger than positivity. HAPPINESS creates the energy to work harder, produce more, sell more, learn more, and create more.

What organization doesn't want that person on the payroll?

@Connie_Podesta:

Professional success starts with a POSITIVE mindset. That's Happiness at work!

#HappinessIsJobSecurity

2

HAPPINESS
KNOWS
ITS OWN
STRENGTHS

Our strengths are the things we were born to do. Love to do. Have a talent for doing. Feel passionate about. HAPPINESS knows leveraging our strengths to our best advantage is one of the smartest, healthiest decisions we can ever make.

But what exactly are our strengths? I often ask my clients to list all of the things they do exceptionally well.

It's amazing how many people struggle with this task. They can immediately focus on their UNHAPPY place and tell me all the things they can't do, wish they could do, don't do, are afraid to do, or have done wrong. Those are the first things out of their mouths.

But, for whatever reason, they find themselves unable to describe the value they bring, the talents they have, and the traits that shine and put them over the top. They tell me it feels like bragging or blowing their own horns.

How sad is that?

People are more comfortable listing their mistakes than their successes.

That is really upside-down thinking at its worst. And it's clear evidence of Unhappiness hogging the spotlight.

Believe me, there is a big difference between bragging and being smart enough and savvy enough to communicate your strengths. And use them at every given opportunity!

How exactly does Happiness become the hero in this arena? It can prevent you from falling into the swirling vortex of self-criticism. It can help you remain objective as you identify your unique strengths and talents. And it also gives you the confidence to share information about your best assets without sounding...well, like an ass. Pompous. Egotistical. Pretentious.

Just like companies work to determine and promote their "unique selling propositions"—the things that make them stand out from their competitors—we can gain big career advantages by knowing what really sets us apart. What makes us valuable. What gets us noticed.

Bottom line:

Figure out what you can do really well, what you love, what you enjoy, what comes naturally. What job truly makes you happy?

Know your strengths. Then graciously let other people know what you have to offer.

You'll be amazed at how that clarity will help you match your strengths to the right job, the right person, and the right lifestyle.

Now that's a **formula** **FOR** SUCCESS.

@Connie_Podesta:

Happiness helps you match your STRENGTHS and PASSIONS to the right job for career success.

#Happiness4Success

3

HAPPINESS
IS ASSERTIVE

Assertive communication comes naturally from a HAPPINESS mindset.

Let's start with some context. Assertive means letting others know your needs, concerns, and feelings in an open and honest way. Without game-playing, gimmicks, threats, manipulations, or hidden agendas. Wow! Wouldn't that be a great way to converse with people all the time? In the conference room or the living room.

Liberating. Refreshing.

Unfortunately, communicating assertively is not so easy. It requires a high level of confidence and self-esteem to be so honest and forthright. Too many times, people resort to manipulation to get their needs met instead.

UNHAPPINESS uses some basic emotions to manipulate others: HURT, ANGER, and GUILT.

You know the types. There are those passive people who use HURT—*whining, complaining, and playing the victim*—hoping to make us feel GUILTY enough to give in to their demands.

Contrast that with their more aggressive counter-parts. These are the folks who use ANGER—*threats, yelling, sarcasm, and put-downs*—with the goal of intimidating us into giving them what they want.

UNHAPPINESS also loves to be passive-aggressive, which delivers the super-sized combo platter of HURT, ANGER, and GUILT. Passive-aggressives are all about getting even while drawing you in with a smile and a wink. Teaching others a lesson. Gossiping. Tattling. Withdrawing love and affection. Giving the silent treatment.

All of these are unhappy moves that cause others to suffer without ever identifying the problem and working toward resolution.

Think about it. When you are getting even, nothing good is being gained. No attempts to reconcile or get to the root of the problem are even on the agenda.

HAPPINESS doesn't play these games.

When you are communicating assertively—in a forthright, adult way—you are tapping into your HAPPINESS communication style. And guess what? Happy people tend to get their needs met. Without all the guilt, anger, and intimidation. Wouldn't that be nice for a change? Try it. You'll like it. I promise.

My advice?

Use ASSERTIVE communication to move your career ahead at a faster pace. It will position you as a leader when working with colleagues and co-workers.

Plus, assertive communication will give you a leg up when interacting with challenging personalities, difficult situations, or manipulative behaviors. Unhappy customers. Uncooperative service representatives. Telemarketers who call during dinner. Even feisty two-year-olds and belligerent teenagers. Whoever. And whenever. Assertive communication helps to put you in charge.

Want more HAPPINESS?

Communicate ASSERTIVELY to create mutually satisfying solutions with win/win results.

@Connie_Podesta:

Happiness allows us to COMMUNICATE assertively—and successfully!

#AssertivenessIsHappy

114

4

HAPPINESS
DOES THE
RIGHT THING

That seems like an easy concept to follow, right? So what's the problem?

Unfortunately, UNHAPPINESS wants us to believe that doing the right thing is not always the easiest course of action. It may not produce the fastest results. Or make the most profit in the shortest amount of time.

In a world where short-term results are too often the measure of success, long-term solutions may get lost in the rowdy crowd of do-it-quick strategies.

As a result, shortcuts are being taken. Value, integrity, and word of honor get lost in the shuffle of a crazy, insane world.

STOP!

Reassess this situation.

HAPPINESS assumes doing the right thing is non-negotiable; it is the only choice to make.

Often, people tell me it is hard for them to know what the right choice really is. So the next time you have to make a difficult decision, ask yourself this: am I getting direction from my EGO or my GUT?

Letting our egos control our choices always gets us into trouble. Egos like to gamble on life, do stupid things, bypass the big picture, and definitely make poor choices when it comes to money, jobs, and love.

Trust your instincts. If you have a bad feeling, don't brush it off. Instinct has been around for eons for a reason. It kept us alive.

Nothing good comes from doing something that goes against your values, your beliefs, and your instincts. Doing the right thing is not a sometimes thing—it's an all-the-time thing. It's the cornerstone of personal responsibility and corporate responsibility.

No easy way out on this one.

Let HAPPINESS GUIDE YOU.

@Connie_Podesta:

Doing the right thing is a permanent state of mind. All the time. No exceptions.

#HappinessHasIntegrity

Section 3

5

HAPPINESS
BUILDS
CHARACTER

Our character is measured by how we act when things DON'T go as planned.

It's easy to be kind when life is going our way. The computer is working at top speed. The bills are paid. The day is sunny. We feel great. These are the times when being positive and doing the right thing should be a piece of cake.

But how do we act when things don't go our way? When life hands us a big, ugly mess. When the economy tanks. The deal doesn't close. The car breaks down. Or the project we worked on for the last six months gets cancelled.

When adversity hits and crisis looms—these are the times when our true character shows. This is when others can see the person we truly are.

How do we act when we are tired, stressed, frustrated, angry, worried, sad, or scared? That's when people watch us. Our customers watch us. Our co-workers watch us. Our kids watch us.

Do they see...

confident strength?
Or deflated bitterness?

These are also the times when the mindset we CHOOSE determines how a bad day turns out in the end.

HAPPINESS is a great catalyst for changing negative feelings into energy, creativity, action, results, options, and solutions.

It's the fuel that can help us transform that big, ugly mess into something beautiful. Something useful. Perhaps something even better than we imagined before the chaos set in.

When the going gets rough, take a look in the mirror. If you don't like the YOU looking back, it's time for a CHANGE. And a big glass of character-building Happiness.

Bottoms up!

@Connie_Podesta:

Real character shows up when times are tough. Happiness is the architect to rebuild your spirit.

#HappinessBuilds Character

Section 3

6

HAPPINESS
SELLS YOU
Like Nothing Else Can

If I were to ask about your job description, what would you say? Hopefully every person reading this book shouted out...

"I AM IN SALES!"

That's right. It's unquestionable.

No matter what you do or whom you work for, you're in the awesome and rewarding business of SALES.

Let me explain.

Are you part of a department where you have to pitch your ideas or make your case for getting a bigger portion of the budget? Oh yes. You are in sales. Are you married? Definitely in sales. Are you a parent? That's sales, 24/7. On a neighborhood committee? Sales again.

Sales is not just about selling a product or service. SALES is the art of persuading, motivating, or influencing others to be open to new thoughts, behaviors, attitudes, and ideas. HAPPINESS has an amazing way of being able to turn negative, non-productive, resistant thoughts into positive, creative, innovative ideas and solutions that deliver over-the-top RESULTS.

In fact, Happiness deserves the
top-performing,
quota-busting,
customer-satisfying,
business-building
SALES award. Every. Single. Year.

HAPPINESS radiates pride, integrity, confidence, and a strong vision for the future. UNHAPPINESS exploits ideas and people through manipulation, pressure tactics, intimidation, and guilt. What's your technique?

Remember this:

The **very first thing you must sell** in life is YOURSELF.

People must believe in you before they put their faith in you as an employee, a boss, a team member, a partner, a parent, a friend, a business owner, or a spouse. And people believe in you only when you believe in yourself.

Make Happiness your agent.

@Connie_Podesta:

EVERYONE is in SALES.
And Happiness is the key
to closing every deal.

#HappinessIsATopSeller

7

HAPPINESS
CREATES
ABUNDANCE

People who have chosen a HAPPINESS mindset create their own abundance in life. They believe there are more than enough resources to accomplish what they want. That their success does NOT have to mean others will fail. That the more they give, the more there is to give. The more successful they are, the more they can help, mentor, and teach others to be successful.

It's like living with unlimited data on your cell phone and infinite storage on your computer. Forever. Bask in that thought for a minute. Yes, I'll take the Happy Abundance package, please.

The flip side of that coin is UNHAPPINESS. It thrives on a scarcity mentality: the belief there is a true lack of resources. That we must buy, spend, grab, scoop up, and take as much as possible before someone else snatches it away from us. That's scary stuff.

The scarcity mentality causes people to become territorial, hoard ideas, keep secrets, and concentrate power—all out of fear that someone else might get the upper hand. No wonder so many people don't get what they really want in life. They live in constant fear and, as a result, are never open to other people, other ideas, other ways of thinking, or other opportunities.

So where does ABUNDANCE start?

It starts with YOU giving more. More time. More money. More ideas. More expertise. More energy. More insight. More help.

Begin to share what you do have, and immediately you start to ATTRACT more of what you don't have—yet! Remember that there is NOT a limited amount of success; success can be achieved by anyone who goes after it.

Your competition does NOT have to be your enemy. Take me, for example. I partner with other speakers. We share clients, stories, ideas, and healthy feedback. We share our successes, and it helps all of us to grow, achieve more, and raise the bar. I challenge you to try the same approach.

The fact is, UNHAPPINESS is constantly trying to beat everyone, outdo them, and win at their expense.

But HAPPINESS? That's about sharing the joy, the wealth, the achievements, and the successes. ABUNDANCE takes away the fear and replaces it with a great sense of community, collaboration, and cooperation. Oh yeah—and it DELIVERS more of what you want every time.

HAPPINESS
at its very best.

@Connie_Podesta:

Happiness is understanding
that ABUNDANCE is yours
for the taking.

#HappinessDelivers

8

HAPPINESS CAN HANDLE CHANGE

Our jobs never involve a tidy, cut-and-dried, etch-it-in-stone process. Things change. Customers have new requirements. Budgets get cut. Deadlines move up. New regulations are passed. The whole thing can be a disorderly, borderline-insane moving target.

No problem.

HAPPINESS thrives on change. Change is the variety and spice of life we need to be creative, energetic, fun-loving, perceptive, intelligent, and innovative.

So ask yourself this question: do I deal with change or does change have to deal with me?

Perhaps it's time to change the way you look at... change.

Change isn't just an annoyance put on this earth to make our lives miserable. Believe it or not, change is really a necessity. Without CHANGE, we wouldn't even be here. Change is why we grow, learn, form relationships, move to different places, try new businesses, and experiment with creative ideas.

Change gives us exciting new ways to complete old tasks. We used to rely on paper maps for road trips. Attend local auctions to buy antique furniture. Visit a local hangout to find a potential date. Today, we have GPS, eBay, and Match.com. Change (with the help of technology) has transformed and simplified the way we do all sorts of tasks. It's propelled us light-years into the future.

Happiness is the inspiration for those who invent the big changes in our world. They see a beautiful vision of what might be, and they work toward it with a positive outlook.

Happiness also helps the rest of us as we try to adjust to the changes. Let's face it, sometimes we approach change with an inner touch of resistance or fear. There's often a learning curve as we adapt to change, but Happiness holds our hands through the whole thing. Which is good, since my GPS frequently sounds annoyed and uses phrases with me like "Recalculating" and "Turn around at your earliest convenience."

Organizations today say one of the top traits they look for in an employee is the ability to adopt and adapt to change quickly and effectively. WITHOUT WHINING ABOUT IT!

HAPPINESS is not a fan of whining and complaining.

Not at all. HAPPINESS is all about looking at change head-on and dealing with it. Happiness doesn't fight for the status quo. Or accept business as usual. Or fear innovation. Happiness is what could literally differentiate you from the crowd, so you can STAND OUT as the person others can count on in times of change.

HAPPINESS is totally worth fighting for when SIGNIFICANT CHANGE is headed your way.

So there you have it. We need to figure out how to make CHANGE an intriguing, exciting part of our lives. Or guess what? Our jobs, careers, even our futures could be at risk.

Did that sound too tough? Are you thinking she doesn't understand what I'm going through at all?

I do understand.

I'm right there with you.

Every time I turn around, there's something new to learn. To do. To think about. To figure out. To accept. To do over. To integrate. And I reach for my Happiness card. It helps me focus and keeps me from being overwhelmed.

Change is a constant, so stop fighting it. Embrace it. Happiness is the powerhouse mindset that helps you do that.

Actually, it kicks your butt until you do what you need to do...and change what you need to change.

But Happiness always carries you through the adjustment. And makes it easier.

@Connie_Podesta:

Successfully dealing with change is in your DNA. Happiness helps you tap into that trait.

#HappinessHandles Change

Section 3

9

HAPPINESS
PAYS IT
FORWARD

Truth be told, we can't ever claim that our success is self-made. No one can.

We are changed, molded, inspired, moved, challenged, and influenced by all the people and events in our lives. And I guarantee you that your favorite people—the ones who literally changed how you think, act, and believe—have discovered the power of choosing HAPPINESS as a springboard for their success. In fact, that's probably what attracted you to them in the first place.

Who are those people? A trusted mentor. A compassionate manager. A loving parent. A treasured friend. Their HAPPINESS has seeped into every pore of YOU! You may have thought it was their amazing ability to make money. Or start a new business. Or close a deal. Or get along with people. Or lead others to success. Or love without conditions. But each and every one of those abilities comes from a foundation and spirit of HAPPINESS.

HAPPINESS is what attracted those things to them and what, in turn, attracted you both to each other.

EVERY PERSON, CONVERSATION, CHANCE MEETING are all part of what makes you...**well, YOU!**

I realize there are all sorts of people in your life who have affected you in both positive and negative ways. Some people need to be cherished. Some need to be forgotten. Some need to be loved. Others need to be told, "enough is enough." And others still need to be forgiven.

For the wonderful people who truly made a difference in your becoming the person you are today, don't wait. Make today the day you say THANK YOU. Express your gratitude to each of them, and let them know the real impact they had on your life. Without a doubt, I know you'll make their day.

Now it's your turn to pass along the power.

Pay it forward.

The best way to do that is by modeling the HAPPINESS behaviors you've learned from your mentors, family members, and friends. Show the world that Happiness has courage in tough times. Demonstrate the patience, character, and hope that naturally flow from a Happiness mindset. Live in a way that reflects Happiness to everyone around you. Like a joyful ripple effect that starts with you and continues in ways you can't even fathom.

Paying it forward is a tribute to those who helped you capture the essence of HAPPINESS in your life, and it's a gift to everyone you encounter in the years ahead. And most definitely even some that you won't.

Not a bad way to begin spreading Happiness across the planet.

@Connie_Podesta:

Thank those who made a difference in your life. Then work to be that life-changer for someone else.

#HappinessRippleEffect

10

HAPPINESS
IS PROSPERITY

HAPPINESS most definitely attracts wealth. But perhaps in a different form than you might think.

Money? Sure, HAPPINESS attracts that. But true prosperity is much more than cash. I've met, coached, counseled, interviewed, and worked with all types of people, both rich and poor. And I've learned one thing: money is only a part of what makes them who they are.

Being rich is not just about having money or things or property or objects. The wealthiest people in the world are RICH in mind, body, heart, and spirit.

HAPPINESS knows the difference between a bank account and the ability to accept ourselves, take pride in our accomplishments, create a sense of balance in our lives, and exude gratefulness for living that comes from deep inside.

Prosperity is about wisdom and compassion. Thankfulness and appreciation. Joy and laughter. Strong relationships and love. A healthy body. And the energy and drive to create something special.

HAPPINESS does not spend more than it has and knows when enough is enough.

UNHAPPINESS lives off credit. And buys what it doesn't even need. Or truly want.

Looking for more prosperity in your life?

Happiness is the gateway to get you there. Surround yourself with people you love and respect—and those who love and respect you in return. Live a healthy, focused life. Have a sense of pride in the choices you make.

If you have a job you enjoy, Happiness and prosperity will come easier. But even if you don't, try to find as many opportunities as possible to use your talents. The more you do that, the happier you'll be.

No matter where you work or what you do, bring HAPPINESS along every day. And soon you'll find the prosperity you've been searching for. It was right there all the time.

@Connie_Podesta:

Prosperity is more than a big bank account. It's happy, healthy choices that create a rich life.

#TheProsperity OfHappiness

Section 3

11

HAPPINESS INSPIRES GREAT LEADERSHIP

Let's get one thing clear right from the start. YOU are a leader. No matter what your job description, title, or nametag says. YOU have the power to influence other people in either a positive or negative way. Through your words, actions, and attitudes.

And you know what? As a leader, YOU have a big responsibility to other people.

So what makes a good leader? Come on. Be honest. HAPPINESS probably doesn't enter into that discussion.

In fact, many leaders tell me they see HAPPINESS as a pathetic, wimpy little emotion that has no business in a tough, results-oriented work environment.

STOP!

Oh no, it gets worse.

Others have told me they try to curtail any overt happy feelings at work, so they will be seen as strong, powerful, and in control.

Let's see how those theories play out.

Think of the worst leader or boss you've ever had. Angry, intimidating, unfair, lacked confidence, didn't take charge, played favorites, wasn't a mentor, wouldn't coach, couldn't motivate—and the list goes on. These characteristics don't come from a mindset of HAPPINESS, do they?

People are just not excited to go to work when they have UNHAPPY bosses who are perpetually scowling. Gruffly ordering everyone around. Placing blame. Taking credit for others' ideas.

UNHAPPINESS doesn't create leaders who have the ability to develop great teams. Or inspire innovation. Or exceed expectations. Or empower others to step up to the plate.

Not much of a contest. HAPPINESS is a much better choice in the workplace.

Just to clarify, HAPPINESS doesn't mean we should go around telling silly jokes or making fun of unachieved goals or laughing when sales are down. While HAPPINESS does have a good sense of humor, it's a mindset of STRENGTH. And from that comes the enviable traits we see in the most successful leaders around the world:

- **Integrity.**
- **Fairness.**
- **Decisiveness.**
- **Cooperation.**

- **Collaboration.**
- **Mentoring.**
- **Accountability.**
- **Intelligence.**
- **Courage.**
- **Dedication.**

HAPPINESS also increases employee engagement. Which is huge! Employees need to feel engaged so they can produce more. Sell more. Innovate more. Work as a more effective team. And produce great results.

Bottom line:

When we make HAPPINESS part of our career skill set, we are prepared to make productive, profitable, long-term decisions. Close deals. Lead effectively. Model good behavior. Make smart choices. Share ideas. Find appropriate solutions. Handle change.

Nothing weak and fluffy there, right?

The fact is, there is no way we can lead without respecting and embracing the power of HAPPINESS.

Make HAPPINESS one of the key traits you seek out in the leaders you choose to follow. And definitely make HAPPINESS your own surefire mindset so others will CHOOSE to follow and respect you.

Great leaders are illuminated with a gloriously abundant supply of Happiness. Like a shining beacon that guides their teams and organizations to greater success.

Is your **HAPPINESS** a 40-watt bulb or a Broadway spotlight?

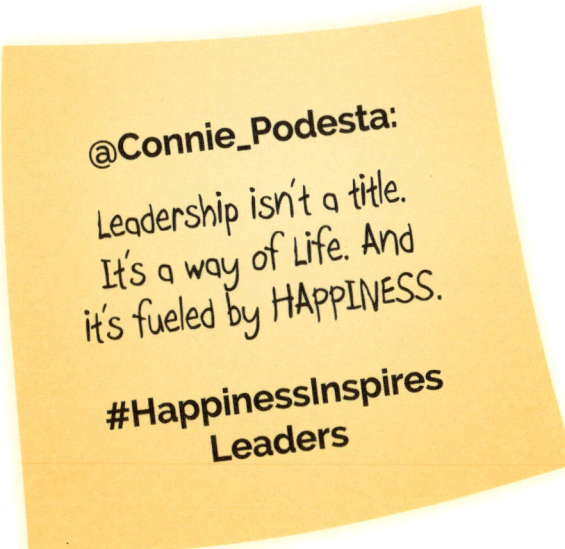

@Connie_Podesta:

Leadership isn't a title. It's a way of Life. And it's fueled by HAPPINESS.

#HappinessInspires Leaders

Section **FOUR**

HAPPINESS:
The **Prescription** for
HEALTH AND WELL-BEING

It's just what the doctor ordered. This section explores the amazing physical impact of Happiness on our bodies. If we aren't healthy, we can't live life to its fullest. And we certainly can't reach the optimum levels of productivity and performance needed to achieve our business goals. Thankfully, a big dose of Happiness comes with healthy side effects.

Yes, you still have to go to the gym. But this is a surprising bonus...

Section 4

1

HAPPINESS
IS THE HEART
OF HEALTH

Research shows that HAPPINESS can absolutely have a positive effect on our health in zillions of ways. Every organ in our bodies thrives on HAPPINESS. It allows us to be calmer, sleep better, work harder, eat healthier, exercise more, and make better choices all around.

How does that happen exactly?

HAPPINESS loves nutrient-dense foods. It goes crazy wild in the presence of vegetables. Fruits. Lean meats. Good fats. It loves to walk. To work out. To meditate. And it loves to sleep. Restorative, restful, rejuvenating sleep. All smart, happy choices that nourish our bodies and give them the very best chance to get healthy and stay that way.

UNHAPPINESS does the exact opposite.

First, it eats junk food and loads up on sugar, starch, and soda. Why?

These processed, nutrient-free foods taste great and feel so good—temporarily. That sugar high makes everything seem all right, until a few hours later. Zap! Down we go again.

And that's just for starters. These foods are literally killers. They douse our creativity, make us irritable and grumpy, and fill us up with wasted calories.

When we make **bad food choices,** we force our bodies to compensate, working overtime with no fuel or nutrients in return. How fair is that? The next time you eat junk, at least apologize to your body.

UNHAPPINESS messes with our minds. It wants us to think food can make us happy. Food can bring us love. Food can make us feel better. Seriously? Are we buying into that garbage?

What about **exercise?** UNHAPPINESS hates it. And has an endless list of excuses to continue binge-watching something on Netflix. Unhappiness is too tired to work out. Too busy. Too sad. Too worried. Too depressed to care about getting healthy.

Sleep is also a big problem for UNHAPPINESS. Too much to gripe about, fret over, complain about. Insomnia creeps in. Cue the tossing and turning. Staring at the ceiling. Calculating how much coffee will be required to get through the 8:00 meeting. And as a bonus, that exhausted, miserable feeling sticks around all day.

UNHAPPINESS wants us to ignore all of the smart things we should do for our bodies. It wants us to eat crap. Stay up late. Sit around. WHY? Because all those things MAKE US FEEL BAD! We'll be mentally tired. Emotionally drained. Physically wiped out.

And when we physically feel bad, Unhappiness can park itself right in the front row of our lives—making us unhealthier than ever.

The cumulative effect is brutal. If we let Unhappiness become a permanent resident in our lives, the long-term outlook for our bodies could be devastating. Illness. Disease. Obesity. Fatigue. Depression. Not a fun club to join.

Bottom line:

If we are unhappy and unhealthy, we're unlikely to get the job we want. Or achieve the success we desire. Or find true love. Or get out of life what we so deserve. Why? Because UNHAPPINESS attracts negativity. Keeps great companies from hiring us. Discourages us from starting a new business. Draws in toxic people. And pushes healthy, awesome people away.

Remember:

HAPPINESS
has to come first.

Is it time for a healthy change of pace in your life? Ready to try the HAPPINESS plan instead of the UNHAPPINESS diet that feeds you illness, anxiety, and insomnia?

Then start now. Give your body what it needs. Walk. Move. Stretch. Eat foods full of vitamins, minerals, and nutrients. Sleep.

HAPPINESS thrives on TAKING CARE OF YOU.

There's scientific proof, by the way. Happiness can statistically lower our blood pressure and improve our heart health. It can reduce our stress. It can give our bodies a boost to release more of the all-natural endorphins that make us feel great. It can strengthen our immune systems. Help us avoid getting sick—and recover faster if we do. Even reduce our risk of disease.

And here's the kicker.

Are you ready for this?

Long-term research even showed that study participants with higher levels of Happiness lived 7-10 years longer on average than the less-happy crowd. That's a jaw-dropper, right?

It sounds impossible—but it's true!
You still get to make the choice: Happiness versus Unhappiness.

Knowing that Happiness could significantly improve your health and potentially increase your life span should make the decision a little easier.

What's your pick?

@Connie_Podesta:

Happiness takes care of you like nothing else can. Your body. Your heart. And your health.

#HappinessIsHealthy

2

HAPPINESS
IS AMAZING
BRAIN FOOD

Our brains LOVE it when our MINDSET OF CHOICE is Happiness. It means all systems are go! Our bodies can connect, communicate, and thrive. It gives us the ability to take positive action, create new ideas, find solutions, and make choices that propel us to success.

The flip side? Unhappiness is rooted in anger, worry, blame, distress, and sadness. And guess what?

These are the toughest emotions for the brain to process.

They suck up all the brain's bandwidth and leave the body to fend for itself. Every organ in our bodies has to make way for those emotions and pull out all the stops to keep going. Those emotions take a huge toll on our bodies' resources.

When our brains are so full of dealing with all the Unhappiness, there's no room left to create a positive thought, master an imaginative idea, or reach out to someone we love. Unhappiness literally robs us of our energy and, consequently, any chance to succeed.

If we want to live healthier, happier, and longer, we've got to nip those negative emotions in the bud, tell those unhappy thoughts to take an unusable rain check, and focus on the inner strength of a Happiness mindset. Because that's our only shot at firing up our brains to do the things we need them to do most— to keep us alive, well, healthy, alert, focused, and ready to cope in bad times. Oh, and leverage the good times, too.

"But just how can I 'nip' a negative emotion and stop it from taking over my mind, body, and soul?" you ask.

This is where the fighting part comes in. Let's face it—an UNHAPPINESS mindset is so easy. Just sit back and let it have its way.

Unhappiness will wash over you. In an instant. And you'll never even know what hit you. It oozes into every cell of your brain, and it uses all your attention and energy to focus on every bad thing that has happened to you. Everything you've done wrong. Hurtful times. Past losses. Shameful experiences. Regrets.

All of a sudden, there's not a healthy, joyful, positive thought left in your head.

Think of it like this:

Unhappiness plays havoc with your subconscious. It puts you at war with your feelings. Armies of un-happy thoughts are attacking you with everything they have. Your brain is surrounded.

So do you just surrender? Slide into negativity? Wallow in despair?

OR DO YOU FIGHT BACK?

Do you give up at the first sign of things gone wrong or do you challenge the feelings that threaten to overwhelm you? What to do? Anything? Something?

Just taking one tiny step toward recovery will give your brain the fuel it needs to fight back.

> *Can you—even in the midst of setbacks—conjure up the ability, willingness, and determination to dig deep and search for reasons to find a tiny sliver of Happiness?*

> *Can you allow yourself the promise of better things to come?*

> *Can you give yourself permission to stop the suffering?*

> *Can you give yourself a break?*

Can you choose to not be angry or sad the rest of your life?

Can you help Happiness help you?

If you can answer "yes," then believe me—it will make all the difference in the world.

Does that sound like a silly list of stuff to do when you are facing unbelievable challenges? Maybe. But it doesn't matter.

It's not WHAT you do. It's that you CHOOSE to DO something—anything—to break the cycle of Unhappiness. Even if only for a minute. Five minutes. An hour.

It's the act of choosing a different mindset. Telling your brain to go the opposite way. To walk away from the disappointment. The pain. The fear. The anxiety. The anger. The sadness.

It's refusing to let that negativity own you. Swallow you up. And destroy your chance of ever being happy again. It is your conscious CHOICE to begin to stop the cycle of Unhappiness. Just try it.

HAPPINESS
only **needs** a foot in the door **to win you over.**
HONEST!

@Connie_Podesta:

Need better focus? Feed your mind with the super-charged vitamins and minerals of Happiness.

#HappinessHas BrainPower

3

HAPPINESS HELPS HEAL THE BODY

Too sick to be happy?

When we aren't feeling well, Happiness can be the LAST thing on our minds. Working our way through the second box of Kleenex. Struggling with back pain. Recovering from surgery. Reeling from a cancer diagnosis. Not much to be happy about there.

The truth is...

A **HAPPINESS** mindset can be **strong medicine.**

Studies show that Happiness works at the cellular level. It can crank up our infection-fighting antibodies to fight germs. Energize our immune systems. Reduce our sensitivity to aches and pains. Help us recover faster.

In other words, we need to keep HAPPINESS right beside us, along with the aspirin, juice, and thermometer.

Seriously, Google it.

Mind. Blown.

Without a doubt, a positive attitude can help bring an illness to its knees (or at least tame its intensity and duration). If you or a loved one is experiencing a serious illness, keeping HAPPINESS in your arsenal of remedies can't hurt at all—and it usually helps.

When my good friend was diagnosed with cancer, I marveled at her courage and her ability to fight for every glimmer of Happiness, even in the midst of turmoil. Fear. Distress.

Was she worried? Absolutely.

But she was determined to keep a positive spirit because she knew without a doubt that her recovery depended on it. She purposely focused on what was GOOD about such a BAD situation. Some days it took extraordinary willpower, but she was truly happy they caught the cancer in time. She was proud she had been taking good care of herself, so she had an immune system in place to fight the battle ahead. She appreciated her outstanding doctors. She counted her many blessings—that she was loved and supported by family and friends.

She wisely knew that negative emotions such as fear, worry, depression, and anger were not going to help her in the months ahead to get well. To fight the best fight, she needed Happiness on her side. She needed to be at her BEST mentally and emotionally so she could get well physically.

Smart lady.

My best prescription for finding the right answers, resources, doctors, and protocols that can restore good health? HAPPINESS.

It may be as close to a miracle as you can get.

@Connie_Podesta:

Happiness can be a strong weapon in your fight against illness, injury, and disease.

#HappinessHeals

4

HAPPINESS HEALS, EVEN IN GRIEF

Grief is...devastating.

Based on my years working as a therapist, I can tell you this for sure: grief isn't something we "get over." We can't simply work hard to arrive at a grief-free place. Deciding to face reality is one thing, but grief is usually still there somewhere, staring us down.

Even when we do move forward, grief actually becomes a living, breathing part of us. We somehow absorb it into our personalities. Our hearts. And our souls. Perhaps a less prominent part as time goes by, but it's always there. Which makes it frustrating when well-meaning people encourage us to recover and get on with our lives. Grief doesn't work that way.

But that, my friends, is where HAPPINESS comes in.

That got a raised eyebrow, didn't it? It's hard to even imagine embracing a mindset of Happiness when someone we love is no longer in our lives. It seems so wrong and out of place. Unnecessary and irreverent. Even selfish and inconsiderate.

But the truth is...

Even in the midst of grief, there can still be so many things that make us smile, memories that can turn tears into laughter, and wonderful stories that will keep the people we love alive forever.

Here's how it works.

Studies show that the intensity of the original grief as a result of a loss, disaster, or trauma may stay the same. But as time goes by, the duration of the intense grief feelings becomes shorter. And the time between the episodes of grief becomes longer.

Happiness is waiting for us right there, in those increasingly bigger mental spaces. It doesn't try to prevent us from grieving or invade our process. But it does carry us through the times in between to keep us living with intent and purpose. It gives us a touch of much-needed perspective. And more importantly, the powerful drive to celebrate life—even though it will be a vastly different life—instead of simply mourning loss.

When our father died, my sister and I decided to make his funeral a HAPPY event. Tearfully happy is probably a better description. After all, our dad could be quite the comedian. We asked everyone who spoke about him to share funny stories, things he had done that they remembered with humor, memories they had of him that still made them smile.

We sang his favorite country songs, showed videos of him featuring his comedic side, and celebrated the pure joy of his unique life. It was the only funeral I've ever been to that got a standing ovation at the end.

In fact, as I stood in the reception line afterward, an elderly man came up and requested my business card and phone number. When I asked why, he said, "Oh, I definitely want YOU to 'emcee' my funeral!"

HAPPINESS had found a way to bring my dad to life again for everyone there. It connected us together in our love for him. And it allowed us to say goodbye with gratitude in our hearts for the years we had with him. Enjoyed him. And loved him. HAPPINESS made the day all about him. Instead of about us.

HAPPINESS can, in its own discreet way, help make the grief bearable.

Often people feel guilty finding Happiness in the midst of grief. As though they are being unfaithful or disloyal. But in truth, Happiness is being grateful for the time we had. And respecting and loving them enough to live our lives to the fullest. Happiness allows the healing to begin. And continue.

The Happiness we shared at my dad's funeral was proof that his life had meaning. It allowed us to remember the good times. And to keep the love alive.

Yeah, that's the kind of stuff Happiness can pull off.

@Connie_Podesta:

Happiness gives us the strength we need to live with our grief and keep memories alive.

#HappinessBefriendsGrief

Section 4

5

HAPPINESS IS GOOD FOR THE SOUL

Happiness is fun.

It's a giggling, cackling, roll-in-the-aisles, hysterical blast of joy. Isn't that what we all need, especially during times when it seems as though nothing could ever make us smile again?

Happiness gives laughter permission to be a staple in our lives. It can make our souls smile. And the health benefits are remarkable.

For starters, laughter relaxes the entire body. Research shows physical tension and stress can be eased for up to sixty minutes after a good, hearty laugh.

Why?

Laughter prompts our bodies to release a big flood of endorphins.

These all-natural, feel-good chemicals have one goal: to help us cope, feel better, relax, and—here's the best part—relieve pain! Now those are some chemicals we all need to tap into. Plus, they are legal, free, and available to us whenever we need them!

Next, laughter helps us keep things in perspective. It enables us to be more spontaneous, less defensive, less inhibited, and more confident. Almost like a glass of happy emotion wine...

How about laughter and relationships? There's no doubt that couples who can laugh together stay together longer and enjoy each other more.

Shared laughter adds a dimension of vitality and joy that helps relationships through good times and bad.

Guess what else laughter can do? It can dissolve UNHAPPY, negative feelings and emotions and help us look at the world from a different perspective.

Think about it.

It is impossible to **frown, sulk, get angry,** or **be sad** WHILE WE ARE LAUGHING!

Go ahead, try it. I'll wait...

So how can you bring more FUN and LAUGHTER into your life?

Surround yourself with people who exude joy and Happiness. Hire them. Work for them. Live with them. Remember, you pick up on all the emotions that surround you. If you hang out with people who are angry, grumpy, whining, disgruntled, bitter, or sad, then guess what? You will be too! Move on.

Laughter and Happiness go hand in hand. Your body and your soul are begging for more!

Fill 'er up...

@Connie_Podesta:

FUN is the heart and soul of Happiness. And it's good for you! So go ahead. Laugh a little.

#HappinessLovesLaughter

Section 5

Section FIVE

HAPPINESS:
The **Secret** to
PERSONAL GROWTH AND SUCCESS

Life is a team sport. This section reveals the winning game plan to improve the way you connect and communicate with all of your team members. At the office. At the kitchen table. At the big conference. Hint: Happiness is the head coach for all of those!

Huddle up. It's game time.

Section 5

1

HAPPINESS IS BY INVITATION ONLY

In other words, **we can't make others feel HAPPY.**

Have you ever tried to make someone else happy? A boss? An employee? A parent? Child? Partner? How's that working for you?

Do they listen, absorb, and scoop up all of your Happiness and good intentions, and then make great changes right before your eyes? Or do they defend, argue, get angry, withdraw, and explain why it just won't work for them? I'm guessing it's the latter.

Maybe you've tried to cajole people out of their Unhappiness with humor. Or bribed them with money, material things, or vacations. Or listened to their ranting and negativity for hours on end, thinking that would help them get it out of their systems. Again, epic fail.

It's easy to get tired of people who are out of sorts, complaining, getting all down in the dumps, or feeling sorry for themselves. We, on the other hand, feel empowered and strong, thanks to Happiness. So we decide we're going to CHANGE THE WORLD. Or at least all the sad, grumpy, angry, depressed souls around us.

But the truth is, we can't make others happy. Props for trying—and wanting to—but...save your energy. It's wasted effort. I see it all the time. Positive, happy people trying to change CHRONICALLY negative, unhappy people. Doesn't work. Trust me.

HAPPINESS only shows up when the individual invites it in. Sorry, an invitation from you doesn't count. Set down the envelope and walk away.

People have to decide when and if they want HAPPINESS in their lives. We can only be there for them and help support them in that decision. Without judgment. Without defensiveness. Without pressure.

Now don't get me wrong. It doesn't mean we have to stay around and be sucked into their black hole of Unhappiness. Or allow their negativity to swallow us up until our own Happiness is lost and struggling to emerge. It doesn't mean we have to take their abuse. Or listen to their constant whining. Or put up with their lack of engagement or productivity.

Choosing to adopt a HAPPINESS mindset is one of the most personal, individual choices we can make.

And we can't help them, force them, pressure them, or beg them to accept that choice for themselves. Or even get them to believe that bringing HAPPINESS into their own lives is a CHOICE.

It would be nice if we could serve the chronically grumpy a big bowl of Happiness and instantly change their attitudes. As a therapist, coach, and counselor, I would LOVE to take HAPPINESS and spread it like a beam of light over and into every person's heart and soul. But I can't.

Take this book, for example. I can speak to Happiness principles, page after page. But how do you react to them? Entirely up to you. If you're not ready, willing, and open to taking them in, adopting them into your life, then they're just words.

Bottom line:

You can't rescue people from THEMSELVES.

Other people have their own journeys to make—even if we disagree with the roadmap. We can love them. Support them. Pray for them. Choose NOT to be with them. Divorce them. Move away from them. Or just accept them.

What about the naysayers and nonbelievers? The grumps and the sticks-in-the-mud? The angry and the disgruntled?

Leave them be. In the end, people decide how to live their own lives. They will either figure it out—or they won't. But you, my friend, have bigger fish to fry.

And here's the catch of the day: since you can't control everyone else, get serious about working to be the best YOU possible. Take care of yourself. Make sure your light, your charisma, and your spirit shine through in everything you do and on everyone you meet. In the boardroom. On the elevator. At the hardware store.

If you want to affect positive change, I say GO FOR IT. But do that by seeking out like-minded people. You'll do more good by modeling HAPPINESS than by forcing it down someone's throat.

By setting a positive example, you could inspire others to invite Happiness over for dinner.

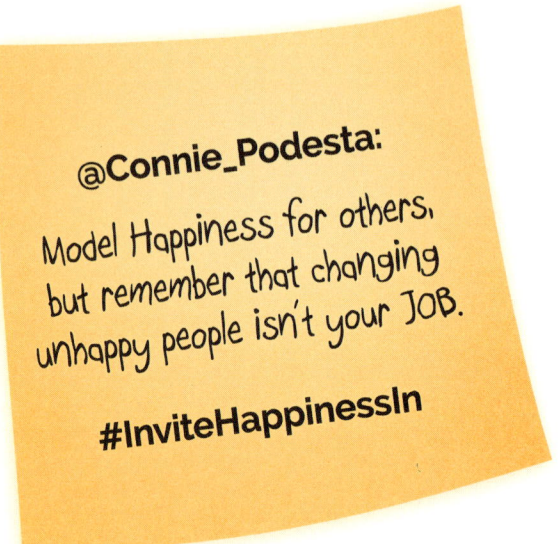

@Connie_Podesta:

Model Happiness for others, but remember that changing unhappy people isn't your JOB.

#InviteHappinessIn

2

HAPPINESS DOESN'T SETTLE

When people believe a promotion, true love, more money, or a bigger house is the thing they need before they can be truly happy, they invariably SETTLE for less—to get what they want quicker! The timeline somehow becomes more important than the result, so they compromise.

How sad is that?

But it's oh-so true.

In their attempt to find the solution to their Unhappiness, they grab the first thing that comes along. And they rationalize all the while about how it may not be exactly what they wanted, but...

But what? That it's better than nothing?

When you honestly begin to realize this HAPPINESS thing all depends on YOU—*not on other people and other things*—you won't ever settle again. Settling is refusing to fight for what you want. Refusing to fight for what you need and what you deserve.

Is that a choice you want to make?

I know sometimes settling seems EASIER. It's the shortcut. The "bird in the hand," as they say. It's taking a promotion we don't even want, because we hope the better title brings us the validation we need at work. Or it's buying a house we don't really like, rather than saving more money for the one we love.

It's choosing a partner who is not the right fit. A partner we may not even like or enjoy or respect. But we think having this partner is better than being alone.

Let me underscore that point before we move on. Don't ever confuse loneliness with being alone. Sometimes it's lonelier being with someone who is not the right fit or doesn't like you or doesn't treat you well than it is to just be alone. On your own. Making your own way. Trusting in yourself. And being happy with who you are. And the power that you alone can bring to the table. That's important stuff; I'm giving you a virtual "high five" right now.

If we're unhappy and we settle, we just keep trudging through, day after day, without ever stepping up to the plate and daring to forgo what's being handed to us and going for what we really want. Because that would be way too risky.

Know this...

SETTLING
almost invariably **means losing. Giving up. Giving in.** And **leads to regrets. LOTS OF REGRETS.**

Section 5

Want more? Deserve better?

Go for it. Don't settle. Choose Happiness and go get what you really want.

Starting now.

@Connie_Podesta:

No more settling. You want and deserve more. Happiness will help you go get it!

#HappinessDoesntSettle

3

HAPPINESS
MEANS LOVING YOURSELF FIRST

Oh, I can hear many of you now.

That sounds so selfish, conceited, narcissistic, or downright egotistical.

Surprise!

Loving yourself through HAPPINESS doesn't qualify for any of those harsh terms.

It's true. If we aren't HAPPY, then we CANNOT be all of the things we need to be to help the ones we love. The people we manage. The friends we cherish. It starts with us.

HAPPINESS makes us a better leader, colleague, partner, parent, friend, sibling, daughter or son, and spouse. There is no place in life—no situation, no relationship, and no problem—where HAPPINESS won't help get us to a better place.

Sorrow, grief, fear, anxiety, disappointment...all of these things can be given a chance to lessen and heal if HAPPINESS is the spark that grounds us. But we must love ourselves, take care of ourselves, nurture ourselves, believe in ourselves, be aware of ourselves, accept ourselves, give ourselves a break once in a while, and consider ourselves IMPORTANT enough to deserve the best.

In this situation, yes! IT IS ALL ABOUT YOU.

YOU have to make yourself the number-one priority. Love yourself first. Respect and appreciate yourself first. Be proud of yourself first. Be good to yourself first. Be kind to yourself first. Happiness helps you get the order right.

Putting yourself FIRST is NOT selfish—it is absolutely the most loving gift you can give to another human being. When you are OK, you give them permission to be OK as well. Your confidence, creativity, hopefulness, encouragement, and positive energy become the FUEL that can give others a jumpstart on living a HAPPY life. And loving themselves!

How cool is that?

@Connie_Podesta:

You can't help others to be happy if you aren't happy first. Make it a priority!

#HappinessStartsWithMe

Section 5

4

HAPPINESS
ISN'T PHONY

Unfortunately, many people confuse HAPPINESS with sugary, fake, over-the-top silliness. Nothing is further from the truth.

HAPPINESS isn't phony. Or fake. Or contrived. That's not to say there won't be times when we have to put on a positive face even though we don't quite feel like it on the inside. But that's being smart—not phony.

HAPPINESS doesn't mean we are always smiling. Or laughing. Or dancing. Or having fun.

197

HAPPINESS is like the foundation of a house.

The house can be torn apart by wind, aged by the sun, or falling down from neglect, but the cement foundation stays put. It forms the base from which the house can be rebuilt, even remodeled and renovated.

TRUE HAPPINESS is definitely AUTHENTIC.

As real as real can be. Remember, it is a mindset, not a phony cover-up hiding our true feelings. HAPPINESS is our emotional foundation. A solid place of hope where we can figure out next steps.

I've had to go on stage during terrible, heartbreaking times in my life. But there was still HAPPINESS inside. I was happy to have a job. Happy to have doctors who could help. Happy to have family by my side. Happy to have a mind that could think and plan and work to get things back on track. Happy to know that I could make it through this!

HAPPINESS is a choice to see both sides—the good and the bad. And then to focus on the good. No matter how small. Or how fleeting. Because it is the only way to make it through. With your sanity intact.

HAPPINESS is strong enough to help—no matter what happens. Especially during times when it's all we can do to keep HAPPINESS at the forefront. With Happiness as our support, we have the outlook and energy to decide what to do next, what options are available, and what resources we need to use to get through tough times.

I don't see that as phony. I see that as our amazing first step in getting well. Being OK. Learning to go a different direction. Finding answers that work.

And most of all, ATTRACTING GOOD THINGS BACK INTO OUR LIVES.

Make HAPPINESS "step one" when you are going through tough times. Then watch as step two and three become a bit easier. When you choose to make UNHAPPINESS your first step, you won't have to wait long to see how destructive step two can get. It's almost automatic.

HAPPINESS is the best strategic plan for moving through. The authentic mindset that helps you move up and move forward. Give it a chance.

@Connie_Podesta:

Happiness is authentic and real. And it's strong enough to support you during tough times.

#AuthenticallyHappy

HAPPINESS
DOESN'T SIT ON
THE SIDELINES

HAPPINESS is NOT passive.

It doesn't wait around to say what it feels or needs.

Many people are so afraid of losing the game that they don't even sign up to play. They sit on the bench, watching from afar, wishing they were on the field, but secretly glad they've escaped the competition of life.

What good will that do? Happiness has a gutsy, bold, go-for-it attitude that encourages you to get in the game!

Don't quit before you even begin.

Don't refuse to sign up for life

because you may not come in first.

Don't be afraid to speak up

in the meeting or volunteer for the challenging assignment.

Don't walk away without trying

because you're afraid you might not get the job, the promotion, the love of your life, the blue ribbon, or the house you love.

Truth is...we might NOT get any of those things. But we will gain insights from what we do or don't do, and we can apply that knowledge to our next attempt. That's how we learn.

UNHAPPINESS doesn't want to take any risks. It waits for everything to be perfect before it puts itself out there. And guess what? Nothing...is EVER perfect. The time is never risk-free where we are guaranteed to succeed.

UNHAPPINESS doesn't even suggest a restaurant or movie because...it might not be the right choice. And that might make someone angry or upset.

HAPPINESS is rooted in confidence. So what if the restaurant is horrible? Now we know. And what if the movie is a rotten-tomatoes-level flop? Next time we will pick a different one. In the big scheme of life, it's not the end of the world. NO BIG DEAL.

HAPPINESS is a mindset that gets us through the good and the bad. The successes and the failures. That's the amazing power of HAPPINESS. It creates a healthy, positive baseline from which we have the courage to try new things, take risks, and put ourselves out there.

HAPPINESS also gives us the confidence to know we will be OK even when things don't go our way or when life isn't fair. Because we all know, it's not.

It may take a lot of tries before you get what you want. Don't sweat it! That's just part of the deal. But sitting on the sidelines afraid to play? That gets you nothing but Unhappiness.

Go on, get in the game.

Ready. Set. Go!

@Connie_Podesta:

HAPPINESS is not a spectator sport. It's your turn to play!

#HappinessGets InTheGame

6

HAPPINESS
FORGIVES

Forgiveness is not ever, ever, ever about the other person. It is all about YOU.

It's about letting go of someone else's power over you. It's about making a CHOICE to move on, push ahead, and allow your own future to take shape WITHOUT the input, memories, abuse, unfairness, or hurtful messages of those who have wronged you. It's about choosing HAPPINESS.

Difficult, I know. We can talk all day about how awful these people who hurt us might be. Or how misguided, wrong, stupid, cruel, even sick. But is that what REALLY MATTERS?

Learning WHY they did what they did (or said what they said to you) rarely releases you from the hurt, pain, anguish, sadness, fear, or downright unfairness of the whole experience. UNHAPPINESS doesn't want to budge.

The **only thing** that can **RELEASE YOU** and allow you the **freedom to move on** is FORGIVENESS.

Know this:

When we forgive, we are NOT condoning or forgetting what those who have wronged us said or did.

Instead, we are CHOOSING to let go of our addiction to thinking about them and our inability to move on because of them. We are choosing to let go of the anger and grief that has started to rule our lives.

Choosing not to forgive is choosing to walk side-by-side with UNHAPPINESS. As the old saying goes, not forgiving someone is like drinking poison and expecting the other person to die. It's just not logical.

Forgiveness clears our brains. Charges up our hearts. And allows us to focus on ourselves. And NOT on them. A much better place for us to be.

But now hear this: HAPPINESS believes forgiving someone and choosing to keep them in our lives are two separate issues. Just because we forgive someone does NOT mean we must remain their friend. Partner. Employee. Spouse.

In some cases, forgiveness does mean a second chance. The chance to move on with that person—in a new direction. With positive hopes and dreams for a better life.

But more often, forgiveness means leaving that relationship behind. And along with that relationship, we leave behind the hurt and anger that could only drag us down in the years to come.

Forgiveness allows us to FEEL FREE and experience HAPPINESS again. We have the right to CHOOSE Happiness over shame, pain, and sadness. And let's not forget that the person we need to forgive most is frequently OURSELVES.

We could have been better parents. Better managers. Better daughters or sons. Better friends or siblings. Better spouses or partners. We made mistakes. Let someone down. Betrayed a trust. Gave up too soon. Didn't try hard enough.

STOP!

HAPPINESS is forgiving—and that starts with YOU!

208

@Connie_Podesta:

Happiness doesn't HURT.
It FORGIVES. It empowers.
It releases you.

#HappinessForgives

Section 5

7

HAPPINESS
Has No Room
for VICTIMS

Many people fight for the right to be unhappy because they want to continue to play the victim. Why? Because it provides them with an opportunity to make excuses, feel sorry for themselves, blame the past or other people, rationalize poor choices, and justify inaction.

Without all those excuses, they might have to show up, put out some effort, do the work, and risk failure.

Not great options for those who have allowed Unhappiness to camp out on their couches.

When you decide HAPPINESS is your go-to MINDSET, it changes the way you think, behave, and believe— both inwardly and outwardly.

It also changes the way other people perceive you. React to you. Care about you. Feel about you. And choose to relate to you. Once you adopt a mindset of Happiness, people's codependent and enabling behavior toward you STOPS.

It's like rebooting the relationship.

They no longer feel a desperate need to pity you, endure your complaints, tolerate your unhealthy moods, or rescue you from facing life's challenges head-on. Instead, they stand back and offer asser-tive, healthy support when necessary. They know you pretty much have your life under control—even during tough times.

They also like you more. Want to be with you more. Love you more. Have more fun with you. And respect you more.

212

Wow! **Isn't that worth a change in mindset?**

Truth is...

No one wants to be around a chronic victim. It is exhausting. And irritating. And tedious.

Relationships based on Happiness are amazing. Fun. Loving. Supportive. And long lasting.

But if you really like to play the tortured-victim, woe-is-me card, HAPPINESS gets in the way. That's why so many people push Happiness to the curb.

Happiness requires us to step up to the plate and be accountable. Make good choices and own them. Expect the best from ourselves at all times. Stop living in the past. Quit blaming others.

It requires us to totally take charge of the future and do what it takes to get what we want from life. It plants each of us squarely on our own two feet and says, "Get on with it! This is YOUR life. Now make it what you want."

There's a whole new victimless world out there for anyone who wants it. Happiness wants you to take it!

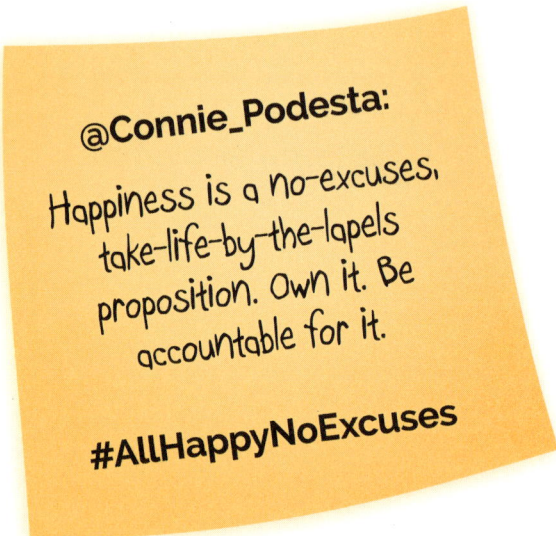

@Connie_Podesta:

Happiness is a no-excuses, take-life-by-the-lapels proposition. Own it. Be accountable for it.

#AllHappyNoExcuses

8

HAPPINESS
DOESN'T
RUN LATE

Late is rude. Thoughtless. Selfish. And excuses don't cut it. I'm not referring here to someone who is late once in a blue moon. I'm talking about someone who is always late. Chronically late. Every day. Wasting everyone else's time.

If that sounds like you, just STOP it. Figure out where you are supposed to be. Back up the time. Do what you need to do. And then get there. On time. Make it happen.

UNHAPPINESS loves rolling in late. And doesn't even care.

It's a power thing. A lazy thing. A disrespectful thing. It silently tells your co-workers, friends, and family that you don't value their time. That it doesn't bother you when they have to constantly wait for your arrival.

HAPPINESS understands the impact of that underlying message and makes every effort to avoid sending it. Happiness strives to be courteous. Considerate. Conscientious. On time. Every time.

Come on. Minutes count. Time is valuable. And a lack of punctuality is inexcusable.

Set the alarm on your phone or your computer. Program your online calendar to send you alerts. Whatever you have to do. Just get to your meetings on time. Your dates on time. Your calls on time. Your life on time.

Enough said.

@Connie_Podesta:

Happiness is punctual.
Be on time for your life.

**#TheHappiness
OfPunctuality**

Section 5

9

HAPPINESS
IS SEXY

Not what you were expecting? Oh yeah...HAPPINESS is sexy! No doubt about it.

When we embrace the mindset of HAPPINESS, we radiate POSITIVE energy to everyone around us. And as a result, we definitely feel sexier. Look sexier. Act sexier.

How great is that?

This is one of the most extraordinary things about HAPPINESS.

Section 5

When we're happy and comfortable with who we are, that changes our physical appearance for the better.

We don't just feel healthier; we look healthier. And there is nothing sexier than someone who radiates clean living, good health, great energy, a confident demeanor, a loving spirit, and a generous heart.

How SEXY is all of that in one package? And we haven't even mentioned the impact of a shining personality, captivating laugh, and a fun sense of humor.

In our Happiness mindset, we make smarter food choices. Take better care of ourselves. We are more content with life. We feel ready to take charge. We are open to new ideas and opportunities.

We look in the mirror and love what we see. Sure, the wrinkles are still there. The laugh lines and cellulite may be visible. Those extra pounds haven't magically disappeared. But thanks to Happiness, we also see a glowing face. A radiant smile. And an aura about us that shouts to the rooftops: "I'm in love with life!"

That is beautiful.
YOU ARE BEAUTIFUL.

Happiness not only makes us more attractive; it makes us downright irresistible.

Many couples who came to me for counseling had literally stopped touching, hugging, cuddling, and even being romantic.

Why?

Because they didn't like themselves. And then they stopped liking each other.

And when you don't like who YOU are, it is very hard to be loving, warm, and nurturing to someone else. Happiness has the power to turn that around.

Sexy means YOU enjoy looking good—not to impress others but because it makes you feel special.

Sexy is sitting outdoors with a cappuccino, watching the world go by. A whiff of cologne with a fragrance you love. A touch of sun on your face. A flirty piece of jewelry. A sunset that never ends. A new outfit that makes you smile. A healthy body. A walk in nature. A twinkle in your eye that hints of fun and laughter. A joyful stride when you walk. A promise of excitement in your personality. And a healthy confidence that attracts others because YOU are a delight to be with, know, and love.

Nothing is **sexier** than a **person who radiates** HAPPINESS!

@Connie_Podesta:

Happiness IS sexy. It's confident, exhilarating, alluring, and sensual.

#HappinessIsSexy

10

HAPPINESS
IS A FAMILY
MATTER

When I ask parents the #1 thing they want for their children, the answer is usually some version of this statement:

> *"I want them to be HAPPY. And I'm going to do everything possible to make that happen."*

My advice? Stop it! As we've already discussed...

we can't make anyone else happy—including OUR OWN CHILDREN.

I know that may be hard to hear, but it's a cold, hard fact. So what can we give to our children that's even BETTER?

Start here:

Give them the tools they need to discover HAPPI-NESS within themselves, all on their own. Now that is a gift for life.

Often in our attempts to give children what we didn't have, we forget to give them what we did have. When I first started speaking, parents wanted different things for their children. They wanted them to be hard working, to never give up or quit just because the job was hard. They wanted their children to be respectful of themselves and others. And they wanted them to be compassionate and considerate of others' feelings.

Those are awesome ideals that still apply to our own children today. We are, unfortunately, in an age where parents want to save their kids from consequences, rescue them from life's lessons, and make them happy at all costs. Sadly, the Helicopter Parent syndrome is a real thing.

Rescuing our children from anything and everything creates insecurity and does NOT promote HAPPINESS. In fact, while it may keep them from experiencing negative consequences, it also prevents them from learning the lessons they NEED about what really happens when they make poor choices.

Didn't finish the paper? Your grade is an F. Skipped school? Sorry, not eligible to play in the big game. Speeding ticket? Better work overtime to pay for it. Consequences aren't fun, but they are a remarkable teacher.

Children who learn from those valuable life lessons grow up to become responsible, accountable, dependable, hardworking young men and women. Which is much more important than becoming adults who feel entitled to HAPPINESS without putting in the effort.

Giving in, giving up, and **giving out to your children** does **NOT bring them HAPPINESS.**

The key:

Model hard work, respect, and compassion for your children through your own life, actions, and attitudes.

Let them see for themselves what HAPPINESS looks like. Feels like. Sounds like. We can't fully teach our kids through words. HAPPINESS shows itself through actions. And feelings.

Want to do something really special for your children? Give them the gift of learning the tools necessary to meet the world head-on, no matter what is thrown their way. Let them know that, instead of someone else rescuing them, they have the power to rescue themselves. To make their own choice for Happiness.

Unconditional LOVE never looked so good.

@Connie_Podesta:

Love isn't about MAKING our children happy. It's giving them the tools to find HAPPINESS on their own.

#TheHappinessLegacy

HAPPINESS:
The **Solution** to
TAKE
CONTROL OF
YOUR LIFE

The driver's seat is waiting. Ready to climb in? This section wraps up with final thoughts about using Happiness to take charge of your journey. Advancing more quickly in your career. Loving your time with family and friends. Going after your passion full-speed ahead. You choose the route, but the destination is sure to include success.

Now roll down the windows. Crank up the music. Happiness is riding shotgun, and it's a beautiful day for a drive.

Section 6

1

HAPPINESS
IS ALL THAT
AND A BAG
OF CHIPS

Can you see it now?

HAPPINESS is the MINDSET that can literally make all the difference in the world. From your career to your family.

HAPPINESS is a POWERFUL and SUCCESSFUL life strategy.

It builds character. It's accountable, productive, and fearless. It's authentic. Accepts imperfections. Personifies abundance. It doesn't procrastinate. And it doesn't settle for less than you deserve.

It's great medicine when you are sick. It's grateful for the people who got you where you are. It believes in you, provides balance, and helps you make good choices.

It allows you to stay in control of your life and impacts your future. It's a key ingredient to your job success and your leadership potential.

Happiness embraces change. It creates healthy, happy relationships. And it is fun-loving and sexy! What more could you ask for?

HAPPINESS has it all. And it's yours for the taking.

@Connie_Podesta:

All good things in life
are rooted in HAPPINESS.
Love. Success. Wealth.
Health. The Works.

#TheHappinessStrategy

Section 6

HAPPINESS
WANTS
NOTHING
FROM YOU

But it wants everything FOR you!

How amazing is that? Just try and think of one other person or thing in your life that doesn't want something. Need something. Ask for something. Or take something from you.

So much in life is about taking.

Think about it.

Unhappiness takes everything from you. It is a narcissistic, selfish emotion that demands that you be miserable to sustain it.

HAPPINESS, on the other hand, is a giving emotion. It is a mindset that caresses your spirit. Softens your outlook. Soothes your soul. And delights in your ability to feel even a tiny bit of peace in a crazy, insane world.

It is a gift to yourself. And to those around you. Which is why it's time to learn how to fight to bring the full strength of Happiness into your life.

@Connie_Podesta:

Happiness doesn't want anything from you. It wants everything FOR you.

#HappinessIsOnYourSide

3

HAPPINESS
BELIEVES
IN YOU

And what you do. And how you look. And where you live. And what your future holds.

I come across so many people who seem to lack the confidence and self-esteem they need to move forward, make things happen, reach out, and develop new relationships. I try to figure out what will bring them the sense of fulfillment and accomplishment they seem to be lacking.

Section 6

They will often tell me that they just don't have enough confidence.

So I say to them...

> *"Then fight to bring confidence into your life. Do whatever it takes to gain confidence— starting NOW!"*

Confidence doesn't just happen. In many cases, other people are more accepting, forgiving, and understanding of us than we are of ourselves. Sad, isn't it?

Like everything else that's good and wonderful in our lives, confidence requires us to stand up and want it and fight for it. Believe me, confident people are scared and nervous and worried, just like everyone else.

But they made two major CHOICES that have changed their lives.

1) They have CHOSEN HAPPINESS as their go-to mindset so they can work from that foundation. Which in and of itself nurtures the confident spirit.

2) They FIGHT AGAINST UNHAPPINESS.
They won't tolerate negative self-talk from others OR from themselves! They close the door on Unhappiness to give Happiness and confidence plenty of space to spread out.

Here's the main thing you need to know. Happiness believes in you. Isn't that comforting? It is cheering you on, helping you navigate the rough waters, and leading the celebration when you win. It's your best friend. Your posse. Your squad. Together, you're unstoppable. And confident!

Confidence is highly contagious stuff. Your high self-esteem will always attract other people who are confident and then...WATCH OUT! You now have a powerful team working together to accomplish great things. It is much easier to be confident when surrounded by other confident people.

Unfortunately, even those who claim to want more confidence often find themselves moving into relationships with individuals who are even less confident than they are.

I understand this from a psychological perspective. People tend to feel better about themselves when in the company of those they perceive to be "less" than they are. Less smart. Attractive. Talented. Capable. If that is your reality, then you are letting UNHAPPINESS pick your friends.

HAPPINESS chooses to surround you with people you can look up to. Learn from. Be inspired by. People who won't accept less from you than they know you can give.

If you aren't feeling confident, then find out why. Don't cop out by making excuses or giving yourself permission to feel less than extraordinary. Ask yourself some tough questions.

What is keeping you from accepting yourself as amazing—flaws and all?

What is standing in your way, preventing you from being who you want to be?

What choices need to be made to change your life? What people do you need to get to know? Learn from? Ask for help? Partner with? Stay away from?

Consider those answers and use them as your marching orders. Do it sooner rather than later!

It's critical—for **your career, your relationships,** YOUR LIFE.

And don't be so hard on yourself. Refuse to live one day longer without believing in YOU. It's not healthy. And it's not OK for you to keep feeling this way. Happiness can show you how.

If you're feeling stuck, just do what I do. Play the "confidence" game. Inside, I'm shaking. Outside— I'm a ball of fire!

Developing confidence is hard work. Every day. It requires YOU to be involved and determined to feel good about yourself. Start today. Believe in yourself. And let your confidence begin to grow.

Happiness always has your back.

@Connie_Podesta:

Feel confident! And try to believe in yourself as much as Happiness believes in YOU!

#HappinessHasYourBack

HAPPINESS
COVERS ALL
THE BASES

If I've done my job, I've helped you to begin shifting your definition of Happiness. This little emotion we had all fluffed up and taken for granted really is the number one answer to life, love, health, wealth, and success.

It's not what most people anticipate. HAPPINESS isn't a scrawny, little guy in the corner of the gym. It's actually a heavyweight champion with perfectly sculpted muscles and the ability to bench-press 300 pounds. Hey, I love surprises.

So now, when you think of Happiness, here are four things to remember.

ONE
It's backwards.

Well, the traditional way of thinking about Happiness, that is. It's inside out. We usually believe we'll be happy once we get the job, find the right partner, have kids, make more money. Whatever it is...that's a myth.

The cause and effect roles are backwards. Flip the order, and you'll get the most important message of all.

HAPPINESS isn't the RESULT of getting what you want; it's the CATALYST that makes getting what you want possible.

244

To get what you want—and keep it—HAPPINESS must come FIRST.

And here's the icing on the cake. Once you understand and apply that reverse principle, your HAPPINESS will naturally attract the people and opportunities you need to help you get exactly what you want. At work. At home. And everywhere in between.

Give that a try, and I promise you'll be amazed by the results. You'll find real-world proof that Happiness is so much more than an emotion. It's a power-packed, get-things-done, success-boosting mindset that will change your life, put your career on fast-forward, and open up a whole new world of possibilities.

TWO
It's a choice.

Happiness is an easy "default" mode when everything's coming up roses. But what happens when Unhappiness hits you in the head like a brick?

When adversity and tragedy slam dunk you without warning and you can barely breathe? When disaster strikes? Or you endure a loss that's unfathomable?

You do the human thing.

- **Cry.**
- **Scream.**
- **Hide.**
- **Withdraw.**
- **Sleep.**
- **Worry.**
- **Yell that it's unfair.**
- **Obsess.**
- **Get depressed.**
- **Stop eating.**
- **Eat too much.**
- **Cry more.**

And then...you have a choice to make.

Stay in the deep, dark valley of Unhappiness? Or start climbing out toward something better? Namely, Happiness.

You have the power to CHOOSE. To open up just the teeniest of spaces to allow a splash of Happiness to seep in and start working on your recovery. You make room for your human instinct to summon your resilience, so it can begin to take over. And when it does, it opens up more space for Happiness to grow, giving you a chance to thrive and love and be well again.

Choosing Happiness gives your body permission to do what it was created and meant to do. SURVIVE.

THREE
It's a fight.

Too bad choosing Happiness doesn't have the instant gratification of choosing to have microwave popcorn. Salty snacking in under three minutes. Once you've made the choice to be happy, it can be hard work to get there. It can take some time. And it's usually a FIGHT.

Happiness requires fighting. And fighting HARD. Just as you have to fight for your right to be loved, respected, cherished, acknowledged, recognized, and appreciated.

The point is, know going in that it's not easy to keep HAPPINESS as your go-to mindset. Why? Because UNHAPPINESS is a powerful good-mood blocker, always ready to take you down a path you don't really want to travel.

It's as stubborn as a mule. So if you want Unhappiness to move out, you may have to give it a swift kick in the rear. Subtle just won't cut it.

But once you win the fight for Happiness, it's important to remember how awesome it feels. When it begins to slip away the next time there is a crisis, you will immediately be aware of the changes—in your heart, mind, and spirit—and you will know the importance of FIGHTING to get Happiness back.

Choosing Happiness isn't enough. You have to want it. Love it. Need it. Believe in it. And FIGHT for it.

FOUR
It's a knock-out strategy.

Happiness makes a huge impact—with results that show up in every nook and cranny of your life. It invades every pore of your being. Professional to personal. It's everywhere. You can smell it. Taste it. Feel it.

And there's plenty of proof.

It's a powerful MINDSET that gives you courage, confidence, and hope. Helps you put things in perspective. Allows you to love your imperfections. Enables you to live in the moment. To know when it's time for seizing a great opportunity. Or to let go of something that's dragging you down.

Happiness also provides you with a distinct advantage in your RELATIONSHIPS with others. A big edge in your personal growth. It helps you to be authentic, understanding, and flexible. Forgiving. Punctual. Fun. Did I mention sexy?

Section 6

Choosing Happiness is one of the greatest things you can do for your HEALTH. Research shows that it has an enormous impact on your body. Your heart. Your brain. Your immune system. The Happiness mindset helps you to stay fit, trim, and well-rested. It even reduces stress, which lowers the inflammation that is linked to a wide range of diseases.

Finally, Happiness can be the secret weapon to turbo-charge your CAREER. It's like winning the professional development lottery. When you're happy, you are more assertive. Agile. Resilient. Grateful. You understand the real value you bring to your team and your company. And you can share that value to get ahead in record time. Start your own company. Create a new product. Whatever you do, HAPPINESS will pave the way for success and job security.

You'll marvel at how Happiness opens doors and delivers just the right resources. Customers. Mentors. It inspires you to take on more responsibility. Accept new challenges. Become the leader that others admire.

Amazing evidence? You bet!

So now it's time. Time to adopt Happiness as the power strategy for your career. Your relationships. Your life. Your future.

And, of course, you know the big secret. Just like everything else, it's up to you.

Already happy?

Don't worry, there's more where that came from.

Kinda happy?

Who wants to be mediocre in the HAPPINESS game? Don't settle for a little bit. Max it out.

Not happy at all?

Why? Seriously, WHY?!? Do something about it! That's no way to live your life.

Make today the beginning of something extraordinary. Don't wait!

CHOOSE HAPPINESS.

Adopt the incredible mindset that will change everything. Activate the catalyst that will make success
possible. Fight through the inevitable dark days
to find the promise of a bright, shining future. To
catapult your career. To enhance your personal
growth. To elevate your potential.

Happiness is the solution to help you take control
of your life. Personally. Professionally. Completely.
Research proves it. And you deserve it more than
anything else in the world.

Go ahead; check your watch.

It's definitely time to take HAPPINESS seriously.

@Connie_Podesta:

Rock-solid proof and a jaw-dropping track record: Happiness IS serious business!

#HappinessGetsResults

Acknowledgements

Content Curation and Consulting
by Julie Escobar

Julie Escobar is a professional writer and editor specializing in creative collaboration with speakers, trainers and coaches. Delivering experienced insight and a creative edge, Julie helps her clients to generate greater response, connectivity and results.

www.SpeakersChoiceConsulting.com

Graphic Design and Layout
by Kendra Cagle

Kendra Cagle is an award-winning graphic designer with a Bachelor of Science in Graphic Design from The Art Institute of Fort Lauderdale. She combines creative talents with a passion for art to craft original design for speakers, authors, and fellow entrepreneurs.

www.5LakesDesign.com

Content Development and Editing
by Susan Priddy

Susan Priddy is an award-winning writer and marketing strategist who specializes in targeted business communications that generate real results. Integrating her MBA and Journalism degrees, she is known for developing powerful content infused with strategic focus and creative flair.

www.SusanPriddy.com

More from
CONNIE

Book Connie
to Speak at Your Next Event

Connie will dazzle your audience with an unforgettable experience that generates lasting, positive change. She ignites an amazing buzz of energy and empowerment with her high-octane blend of wisdom, humor, and enthusiasm. Best of all, Connie inspires bold action. She challenges her audiences to defy limited thinking and dare to **STANDOUT!**

Contact Connie's Team
to Check Availability

Call **(972) 596-5501**

or send an email to:
connie@conniepodesta.com

Top-Rated
BOOKS

10 Ways to STANDOUT from the Crowd

Finally! A business book that isn't boring! Awarded the Independent Publishers award for "most visually stunning business book," StandOut is an artistic delight chock full of real-life success strategies that can propel the reader to new levels of success—both personally and professionally. TEN condensed books on the TEN hottest topics facing business professionals in today's changing world. Get ready! This may be the first business book that you really just can't put down!

Life Would Be Easy
If It Weren't for Other People

Imagine what you could accomplish if you could decode the mystery of human behavior and truly understand what makes people do what they do and say what they say.

Human Relations expert Connie Podesta will take you right inside the minds and personalities of the people you deal with every day—bosses, colleagues, partners, customers, friends, and family—so YOU can ACT, rather than REACT, to whatever life throws your way. Get ready for less stress and more success!

Selling to Women / Selling to Men

TWO books for the price of one (back-to-back!). There is no doubt that men and women have very different buying styles. Knowing how to adapt to each gender's preferences is the key to closing more deals and developing long-lasting customers. Discover how to identify the gender-specific needs and motivations of potential buyers and then apply that knowledge to powerfully influence their purchase decisions.

Texting Harry

A true story of courage, change and life's possibilities. Tired and overwhelmed, Harry boarded a flight to Dallas from Boston. He had lost his creative spirit, excitement for new ideas, and passion for adventure. He was ready to give up. Then...he sat down next to Connie. And his life was about to change. The transformation Harry made in the next few hours was remarkable and poignant. We all know someone like Harry—someone who just needs a reminder that we are never too old to get back on track and experience everything life has to offer. This story will warm your heart and bring a tear to your eye. It's a must-read!

Connie's books are available on her website at
ConniePodesta.com.
For information about quantity discounts,
please call **(972) 596-5501.**

Connect with
CONNIE

Phone: **(972) 596-5501**

Email: **connie@conniepodesta.com**

Website: **www.ConniePodesta.com**

Follow Connie

Connie Podesta Presents

Connie Podesta

@Connie_Podesta

Connie Podesta Presents, LLC

3308 Preston Road; Suite 350-119

Plano, Texas 75093

About
CONNIE PODESTA

Connie Podesta is a game-changing, sales-generating, leadership-developing, revenue-building ball of fire. Her rare blend of laugh-out-loud humor, amazing insights, convention-defying substance and no-nonsense style have made her a consistently in-demand international business speaker for more than 25 years.

Two million people. 1,000 organizations. Hall of Fame speaker. Award-winning author. Seven books. Former radio/TV personality. Humanology expert. Licensed professional therapist for 30 years. Executive career, speaking and life coach. Expert on the psychology of sales, leadership, change, communication, and getting your act together! Plus, what we all could probably use in today's crazy world: a comedienne.